Praise for *Wild Soul Runes*

"In recent times, runes seem to have been relegated to the realm of the masculine with many considering Galdr, the practice of rune song, to be a skill used by men. However, these mysteries are open and available to anyone of any gender or cultural background. As evidence of this, Lara Veleda Vesta deftlyreclaims the feminine power of the runes by inviting you to delve into these ancient concepts in your own way through self-inquiry and personal exploration, while keeping one foot firmly rooted in Old Norse wisdom. A recommended read for those seeking the ancient wisdom of runes while exploring their own path of spiritual growth." —Kaedrich Olsen, author of *Runes for Transformation*

"Within *Wild Soul Runes* you will find a thirty-three–week course that embeds your consciousness in the realm of the Runes by immersing you in a rune a week. You are "going under the cloak" to gain a greater understanding of where these symbols come from, including historical context and no less than four translations per rune. Vesta has created the perfect blending of scholarship and personal gnosis to form a complete picture of that rune's teaching and bring the reader wholly into each rune's realm." —Amy Blackthorn, author of *Blackthorn's Botanical Brews*

"In her book *Wild Soul Runes*, Lara Veleda Vesta presents a concise history of the runic alphabet and a powerful workbook for listening to, learning from, and intimately knowing the runes. In this work, the runes emerge as individuals, as *beings*, that, taken together, create a community that imparts transformative wisdom." —Jesse Bransford, clinical associate professor of art, NYU Steinhardt and author of *A Book of Staves*

"Take a walk on the 'wild side' of the runes with Lara Veleda Vesta, as she leads readers on a unique journey *Wild Soul Runes* moves between the subconscious layers of the web of Wyrd to connect to the ancestors by inward journey and meditation, as well as tapping into the mysteries with the aid of the Norns and Gullveig. The weekly rune exercises and ancestor work offer readers a deep and introspective spiritual growth opportunity." —John Hijatt, runester and host of the *Gifts of the Wyrd* podcast

T0021484

"Although I have worked with the ancestors most of my life, *Wild Soul Runes* gave me even more ideas to add to my ancestral toolkit. At the author's suggestion, I took time to write with the ancestors each morning, then paused, giving them time to write back. This advice, alone, was priceless. In addition, the way the author allowed the runes to ask their own questions challenged me to peer into the intersection of where seemingly contradictory energies meet. The questions and the subsequent journaling made the runes far more personal to me than I'd ever felt before." —Nancy Hendrickson, author of *Ancestral Tarot*

"*Wild Soul Runes* is both a well-needed breath of fresh air and an important contribution to contemporary rune knowledge and understanding. It is empowering, comprehensive, and unapologetically free of the patriarchal dogma ever present in so many other rune books. Lara Veleda Vesta takes us on a journey through what is known historically about the runes and then gently encourages and guides us into the unknown, taking the runes back to their feminine source. From crafting your own runes, creating ceremonies and ancestor altars to calling on our Motherline Ancestors to heal generational wounds, *Wild Soul Runes* is at once poetic, thorough, and brilliantly clear. It is now among my top recommended, go-to books for those seeking to begin their rune studies with the runes, as well as those who truly wish to engage with them deeply, developing a relationship and welcoming them into their lives." —Gæbriel Tämäya, author of *White Stones & Little Bones*

"In *Wild Soul Runes*, Lara Veleda Vesta beautifully demonstrates a deep knowledge of the runes and explains their connection to the Divine Feminine. Vesta has created a wonderful practice to deepen your personal journey with the runes. Whether you are an experienced practitioner or a new beginner, this book will deepen your comprehension. We thoroughly enjoyed reading and learning from these pages and know that you will, too." —Amanda Keith and TJ Vancil, owners of *3 Crows Conjure* and *Occult Master Class*

"It is always a good day when a book surprises and delights the reader. Lara Veleda Vesta's wonderful *Wild Soul Runes* is such a book. She has taken the received wisdom on this old system and given it a freshness that I found intriguing. Vesta's work opens this system to those like me who are curious about the runes. I recommend her unorthodox and appealing interpretation." —H. Byron Ballard, priestess and author of *Roots, Branches & Spirits*

WILD SOUL RUNES

Reawakening the
Ancestral Feminine

LARA VELEDA VESTA

WEISER
BOOKS

This edition first published in 2021 by Weiser Books, an imprint of
Red Wheel/Weiser, LLC
With offices at:
65 Parker Street, Suite 7
Newburyport, MA 01950
www.redwheelweiser.com

ISBN: 978-1-57863-739-3
Library of Congress Cataloging-in-Publication Data available upon request.

Cover and text design by Kathryn Sky-Peck
Cover art and interior illlustrations © Lara Veleda Vesta
Typeset in Aller Light

Printed in the United States of America
IBI
10 9 8 7 6 5 4 3 2 1

Contents

Acknowledgments, vii

Beginning the Work, 1

The Runes and Your Fate or "Wyrd," 2
Preparation Week—or Weeks, 13

Your Rune Practice, 21

A Guide to the Weekly Work, 21
The Rune Poems, 22
Making Your Rune Set, 28

The Runes, 41

The Elder Futhark, 43
The Anglo-Northumbrian or Jotun Runes, 123
How to End and Begin Again: My Runic Journey, 157
Runes and Ceremonial Divination, 179
Rune Webs and Reading the Wyrd, 182
Closing the Practice: Sharing Your Gnosis, 186

Appendix A: Timeline of the Runes, 188
Appendix B: Rune Resources, 190
Notes, 198

*To the Nornir and the Dísir, to my ancestors and descendants,
and to the web of support (human and nonhuman) that makes possible
this work. By this and every effort may the balance be regained. ALU*

Acknowledgments

First, to my family: Eric, Xavier, Grace, and Rhea. Thank you for supporting and celebrating my wyrdness. You are always the heart and root of all I do. To my parents, grandparents, my brother, and cousins and their families, and the great extended web of relatives who have raised me and nurtured my connection to ancestry and place through love, I could not be more grateful. All I create is in the service of our connection.

To the friends who have stuck with me through turbulence and the circles who have contributed to my growth and practice, especially those including Margrethe, Kristina, Darlene, Raina, and the steadfast members of the first rune study live gnosis group, Rebecca, Sarah, and Megan, this offering holds your imprint everywhere and your belief in me through it all is transforming.

To Dr. Alka Arora and Dr. Mara Keller at the California Institute of Integral Studies where several parts of this book began as papers in the WSE PhD program, thank you for your compassionate teaching, for giving academic substance to my felt sense, and for enriching my cultural and historical awareness.

To the magical Judika Illes, who first called me on the summer solstice and whose belief in this project made it become, I am so grateful to you and the team at Red Wheel/Weiser for your compassionate support of this work.

To my patrons on Patreon, especially the Dark Goddess Creativity Group, Coven Invisible, and Ancestral Weavers: this book would not have been made without your very physical and essential support, and I am so incredibly grateful to have such a community with me on this journey.

Wild Soul Runes began as a lived practice during a year of challenging transition and illness initiations. My family and I lost all of our belongings to toxic mold, were displaced twice due to the ensuing environmental illness that exacerbated my preexisting Myalgic Encephalomyelitis/Chronic Fatigue Syndrome (ME/CFS) to the point where I became mostly homebound and bedridden. It was a year of grief, dissolution, and the disappearance of critical aspects of my identity: as a university professor, as a PhD student in philosophy and religion. During this turmoil I began offering online classes by donation as a way of sharing my path, reducing isolation, and remediating the losses. It was also where I started finding my own spiritual sovereignty with the runes and began the practice that is this book. Out of great obstacles, a richness of reconnection.

I am fully cognizant of my own limitations, neurologically and academically, in attempting this work. The intention of offering is just that: a gift in process. It is to the ancestors that this effort belongs, imperfect and perfectly made, existing beyond duality, just like us all.

BEGINNING THE WORK

The Runes and Your Fate or "Wyrd"

If you are reading this, you are in the wyrd.

Yes, you read that right.

Wyrd is the source of our English word *weird*, which now means "strange" or "different," but at one time meant "fate, destiny."

According to one interpretation of the Norse poem *Völuspá*, the prophecy of the "prophetess, sibyl, wise woman, witch,"[1] sound was the beginning of the universe. From this fabric, the essence of all creation—known to the ancients as wyrd—was spun whole. Wyrd is alive, it shapes everything: life force, energy, gestation, birth, destruction—it forms everything. From this thread of wyrd comes all that you are. From this thread of wyrd also came the runes.

Runes are beings. Not merely shapes, not only sigils, not just magic. Runes are without an easily identifiable point of origin outside myth.

The word *rune* in Old English is *rún*, "a whisper,"[2] a secret; in Old Norse *rúnar*, "secret, hidden lore, wisdom."[3] The runes are not an alphabet. Those runes we commonly know—the Elder Futhark and the lesser-known Anglo-Northumbrian runes—are only a fraction of the documented symbols in the archaeological record. Most of runic history survives thanks to the potency of sacred art, dating all the way back to the Paleolithic.

In mythic terms, runes are fragments of wyrd, also known as the web of wyrd, the weaving of the cosmos tended by a triple female power, the Nornir, giantesses from the beginning of time. The sacrificial god Oðin reached into the feminine well, Urðarbrunner, the Well of Origin bearing the name of the Eldest Norn Urð, whose name gives wyrd its linguistic root. He tore out a fragment of the wyrd, receiving the wisdom of the feminine source, the runes, living pieces of the living web.

Each rune whispers differently, and working with them is an exercise in simultaneity, cloaking and uncloaking at once. The runes have transformed my life and my perspectives; their stories have enriched my personal mythology and shaped my spirituality. For those to whom they call, the voice is a recollection, the shape a coming home.

But how does one begin working with the runes or deepen into relationship with them beyond magic or divination practices?

The Knowledge Is in You: Unverified Personal Gnosis

The purpose of this thirty-three-week practice is to develop a deep personal relationship with each rune in the twenty-four Elder Futhark and the nine Anglo-Northumbrian runes. The way through this is multiple; there is no one path. What I offer is a scaffold, information, recommendations, and a theory based in my own ritual relationship with the runes. The practice consists of building a rune altar each week, examining the ancient rune poems, investigating personal translation, employing meditation and sacred art practice, and toning the runes in a rhythm. Other ideas introduced include:

- Ancestral connection

- Sitting out

- Creating your own rune set week by week

- The Germanic/Anglo-Saxon Wheel of the Year and holy days

- Traditional rune divination practices as recorded in history

- Making rune webs for wyrd divination

The basis for this practice is the belief that we can all receive direct, divine information. It is not just for a few special people—it is the birthright of all humans. We are so inured to the idea that information must come through specific authorities, we have forgotten how to cultivate our own inner knowing, activate our ancestral magic, and believe in this direct communication.

One of the most important concepts in my spiritual development has been what some call unverified personal gnosis, or UPG. *Gnosis* is a word from the Greek and simply means "knowledge." When I first started studying the runes,

I learned just how little information is actually available about them. I also learned—quite fast—that they were speaking to me directly.

For many ancestral traditions, personal gnosis was a natural extension of relationship with the animate, living world, divinities, the dead, and future descendants. This root in family, community, and the natural world meant gnosis was an ongoing, daily part of life.

This isn't to say there weren't people in prehistoric societies whose roles and practices were those of spiritual authority, just that spiritual communion was not reserved for the elite but available to everyone. It was the role of all in the community to share both ancestral traditions passed on through the generations and also to receive and integrate new insights for personal or collective use.

You have it within you to receive personal, spiritual insight and information from the runes themselves.

We all do.

This book is intended to introduce a practice that will help you hone and deepen your ability to interact with the runes.

There is no one way to do this work, but there are some simple techniques that may help you begin. By understanding the elements of effective ritual, you can craft a practice of new relationship.

The Elements of Effective Ritual

In order to connect weekly with each of the thirty-three runes, we are going to create a daily ritual practice.

Anything done with intention is ritual, but not all ritual is effective—that is, having a transformative or sustaining purpose.

What makes some rituals effective while others energetically fall flat?

Understanding the function of ritual phases empowers even the smallest ceremonies, and having a clear ritual intention roots each rite in purpose.

The elements of effective ritual are as follows:

1. Crafting a strong intention that clarifies the purpose of your ritual.
    What would you like to achieve as you ritualize with the runes? A

ritual intention might be simply to develop a relationship with them. Knowing this is your intention can help you show up each day.

2. Opening. The opening or beginning of your ritual indicates a separation from the known world and entry into the unknown, unconscious, or ceremonial space. An opening might be lighting a candle, saying a word or phrase, or simply taking deep breaths.

3. Initiation or transition. This is the liminal ritual space where you perform symbolic actions that reflect your intent. You might draw the rune you are working with, say its name, ask it questions, or simply meditate with it in mind.

4. Closing. The integration of information received in the ritual and return to the conscious world. The closing is extremely important to efficacy. More time should be spent consciously closing the ritual than opening it. You may wish to repeat your opening actions in reverse but add a thanks or blessing for any gifts received or presences felt.

These ritual elements are part of a cycle: they repeat on a regular basis but are never exactly the same.

Ritual is most effective when it is regular. Remember, anything done with intention can be ritual, and the best ritual is one you will *actually do*. In order for ritual to be consistent, I recommend you investigate opportunities for ritual in your life by looking at what you already do on a regular basis. I call this Ritualizing the Routine.

For example, I am most consistent with my ritual when it is connected with my morning cup of coffee. Coffee is an ancestral drink, so I prepare extra for my ancestors and sit with them at the altar in meditation. Or sometimes I write with the runes or spirits while I drink my coffee. This little ritual follows the pattern I've listed above: I create a ritual intention opening by lighting a candle and orienting myself to the cardinal directions and elements, the sky-universe-sun above and the earth below, calling to my ancestors, the rune I am working with, and any other guides that I feel need to be present. Then I make my ritual acts, the offering of coffee, writing or drawing, sitting in meditation, singing. If my intention is inquiry, I might ask questions. Then I thank everyone present, say words of blessing, acknowledge the directions again in reverse, and blow out the candle.

This whole process takes about ten minutes, though some days I might devote more time. I recommend starting with a ten-minute daily practice—you are welcome to grow it as you wish, but ten minutes a day is the nonnegotiable minimum. I've found that by ritualizing things I already do every day—bringing intention, focus, and awareness of the ritual cycle to natural routines like bathing and coffee—I've been able to maintain consistent ritual in my life.

This is really important when working with spirits, beings, or deities. The threads of connection to many ancient systems of earth-based spiritual knowing are scattered and forgotten, so creating intention, showing up regularly, not abandoning them when things get tough—which, they might . . . but more on this in a moment—are an important part of the work that is daily integrated spirituality.

Before you begin this practice with the runes, make a list of ritual opportunities in your daily life and think about them in the context of what ritual means to you and the elements of effective ritual, so that you have an immediate sense of where your rituals may begin.

Being ambitious is celebrated culturally, but when it comes to creating gentle, transformative relationship-based practices, often less is more. Ritual should be achievable and repeatable. These are soul seeds, spores. Like redwoods and honey fungus, big things start small.

A note on challenge and the runes: The runes are ancient beings. They respond to integrity and ethics. If you have things in your life that are out of integrity, places where you are not being honest; are resisting change; or are not letting go based on fear, guilt, shame, or another patterned emotion, the runes will seek to clarify your path before deepening into relationship.

This can sometimes be uncomfortable, even scary, but I have seen over and over again the runes helping people bring their lives into alignment with a deep ethos. They are supportive, nourishing, and aid us in reordering our own sacred stories to bring about positive change.

When I began working with the runes, my life tipped upside down for years. My family lost our home, and we experienced major custodial issues with all three of our children. It was a painful, difficult time. It was also necessary, and everyone ended up in a better situation because of it. In that time I had to resist my early programming and lean into the unknown.

Later I became very sick with a mysterious illness that left me homebound and bedridden for years. I had to leave my job and my PhD program, was separated socially from the very community that brought me to the runes, and eventually became so debilitated I could no longer read or write. In that time of isolation I had to reach deep into my own gnosis, to listen and open to the wisdom that such initiations can offer.

Eventually, life stabilized. I healed, but I am changed. All of these challenges were rites of passage, reordering my life, reconnecting me with my ancestors, clarifying my purpose and work.

Now I have seen it in others as well. The runes will change your life. They will make your path clear and help to eliminate anything that is not supporting your best outcome. This doesn't mean it will be easy, but it will absolutely be worthwhile. If you feel ready for this kind of journey, I give you the words of the ancient Völva in the *Völuspá*, the witch from the beginning of time whose wisdom illuminates much of our runic journey:

Vituð ér enn - eða hvat?

Know ye yet—or what?

Timing Your Practice—Lunar and Solar Cycles, Ancestral Holy Days

I have found it useful to learn about the lunar-solar calendars of my ancestors and to align my practices with these, incorporating some of their veneration techniques, feast days, and celebrations to enrich my modern understanding of ritual.

The runes have a vast origin, so you need not limit yourself to these Northern European calendars. I offer these based on my own ancestral experience, but you can also ask your ancestors for guidance or use your intuition to learn when to begin.

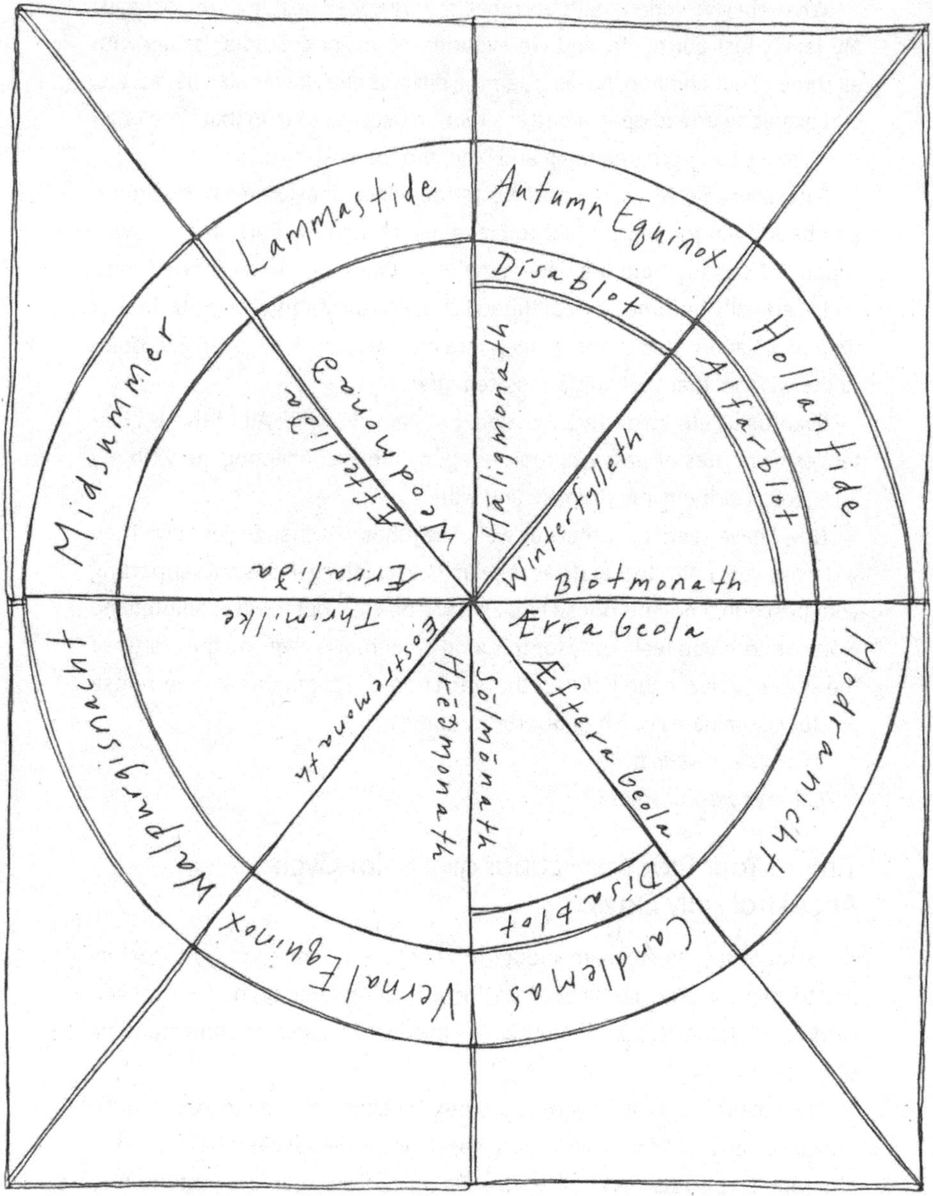
Lammastide
Autumn Equinox
Hollantide
Modranicht
Candlemas
Vernal Equinox
Walpurgisnacht
Midsummer
Dísablot
Alfarblot
Dísablot
Hāligmonath
Winterfylleth
Blōtmonath
Ærra Geola
Æftera Geola
Sōlmōnath
Hrēðmonath
Eostremonath
Thrimilke
Ærra Līða
Æftera Līða
Weodmonath

A few things to note: I am writing from the Northern Hemisphere at a latitude fairly similar to my ancestral homelands and so have a bioregion that reflects many of their rhythms. My ancestral calendars are lunisolar so there are often not exact dates for most festivals. In some reports of Anglo-Saxon and Norse traditions, the year had only two seasons, summer and winter—the concept of a four-season year is relatively modern, but I include it here for reference. In the most ancient ancestral calendars, each day began at dusk the night before, rather than at dawn, which is why so many eves are celebrated (All Hallows', Christmas/Yule)—not as the night before the feast, but rather as the beginning of the feast itself. Similarly, the year begins with the start of winter in October, rather than an arbitrary month in the depths of winter. These wheel markers are included for reference, but are only some of the Anglo-Saxon, Norse, and Celtic holy days by season:

Winter

Winterfilleð: Anglo-Saxon Winter Full Moon, October

Hollantide: Anglo-Saxon All Hallows', Celtic Samhain, the beginning of winter at the cross-quarter day between the equinox and the solstice

Alfarblot: Norse Feast of the Alfar, the male ancestors

Blotmonað: November, month of sacrifice to ensure vitality through the winter

Ærra Geola: Before Yule, December

Modranicht/Winter Solstice/Yule: Mother's Night, longest night

Spring

Dísablót/Dísting: Norse feast of the Dísir, the female ancestors, sometimes combined with the Anglo-Saxon Charming of the Plow for planting season

Solmonað: Anglo-Saxon Month of Cakes, February

Candlemas: Anglo-Saxon cross-quarter day between the winter solstice and spring equinox usually celebrated on February 2, seen as the first day of spring

Hreðmonað: Month of the Goddess Hreða, around the spring equinox in March

Ostara/Equinox/Eostremonath: Month of the Goddess Ostara/Eostre, spring, usually associated with March or April

Beltane: Fire and fertility festival on the cross-quarter day between the spring equinox and the summer solstice, usually celebrated around May 1

Ðrimilcemonað: month of three milks, May

Ærra Liða: Before Midsummer, June

Summer

Liða/Midsummer: Solstice festival in late June

Æfterra Liða: After Midsummer, July

Lammastide: Harvest festival at the cross-quarter day between the summer solstice and the autumn equinox, celebrated on August 2, seen as the first day of autumn

Weodmonað: Month of Plants, August

Autumn

Haligmonað: Holy Month, September

Autumn equinox, Celtic Mabon, considered to be the midpoint of autumn

Dísablót: The second of the Norse Dísir festivals in the year, taking place around the equinox

A Note: Respectful Practice on Colonized Land

I live in North America on the traditional lands of the Multnomah, Kathlamet, Clackamas, bands of the Chinook, Tualatin Kalapuya, Molalla, and many other tribes who made their homes along the Columbia River. Simply learning about my own ancestral traditions and integrating their practices are not enough. To truly honor the land where I live, I need to educate myself about the people of this land in an ongoing, unending, respectful process. If you are reading this in a colonial country, please make an effort to get to know the people of your bioregion and the seasons, plants, animals, and holy days that exist where you live. An animist, living spirituality of relationship is responsive and respectful of both the land and its original inhabitants.

On Nonlinearity and Mythic Time

You may notice there is a nonspecific, cyclic quality to the ancestral calendars. Linearity is one of the myths of modernity: the idea that we progress through living in a particular trajectory. Our experiences are mapped on the arc of these trajectories, and their finality—death, in the case of life, success, failure, learning, not learning, good, bad—tends to be quantified in the terms of duality, another modern myth. But our ancestors lived a rhythm more inclined to the seasons than mechanics, and for our rune practice we too might invite a softening of any linear ideas.

Don't be fooled by the calendar singularity of our seemingly mapped thirty-three-week path. We are traveling in arcs and spirals through mythic time. You may move in and out of the materials and can abandon them altogether in ways that may appear nonsensical, irregular, and bring up emotions of guilt or shame. This happens in all of my classes, and is, in fact, a huge part of my creative process . . . the turning away from rigidity, the returning to experience.

I realize it is because I live in cycle, and this work with the ancients through story, shape, sound, prayer, earth memory, subconscious, magic, is cyclic, too. Were we to make magic a linear path, we would be taxed with the memory of all time, a radiance too great to bear. So we spiral in and out. This is the real gift, for every time we return the opening is wider, and every time we separate from the realm of enchantment, the particles stick to our skin and hair, making luminous our so-called ordinary lives.

So, consider surrender. Consider long walks, music, art, poetry. Consider sovereign acts for the places you love. Consider these the work of the runes, and the whole is blessed, the method yours.

There is no longer room for guilt or shame in our wanderings.

The pace is your own, the work is your own.

You have only to claim it.

Preparation Week-or Weeks

Before embarking on your long practice of daily interaction and inquiry with the runes, it can be helpful to develop space and time for relationship with your ancestors. This can be as little as a week or as long as you wish. By beginning to journey with your ancestors, feeling their presence and creating space in your home with them, practicing some meditation and connection techniques, you can build a strong foundation to aid and support your rune practice.

Ancestral Connection, the Motherline, and the Runes

In ancestral connection I have found it useful to begin with the known—self as mother, mother as mother, grandmother as mother—and weave the way back through thousands of years, tens of thousands, two hundred thousand years to the ancient mother of us all, mitochondrial Eve.

The primordial mother lives within us, present in our cells; they all do, one and diverse. The wombs of the past hold seed cells of the future. My grandmother's womb held the egg that would become me in the body of my fetal mother. My womb held the seed stories of my grandchildren in the body of my daughter. The future nests in the past, simultaneous. This is ancestral connection.

Ancestry is complex. But ancestral connection begins before we even become. And it never ends, looping through time. You are, even at this moment, already connected. We all are.

As we deepen and expand our awareness of inherent ancestral information, new avenues of exploration appear. Beginning with the self is a natural starting point. You contain this knowledge, this wisdom. You contain the tools, resources, and information in this center of intention. Through practice we awaken what is latent and only dormant. We begin with this:

Our ancestors live within.
We awaken to their presence through the motherline.

Why the motherline? All ancestors are important, and throughout this experience you may encounter information from ancestors of diverse or nonbinary genders. My first ever ancestral meditation brought a male relative forward, which surprised me as I had spent years intentionally cultivating experiences with the feminine. We work with the motherline not to exclude, but to repair. We must reweave and absolve thousands of years of neglect to our grandmother ancestors. The well or source of the runes is feminine, so connecting to our motherline can bring us back into alignment with the partnership synthesis between the masculine and feminine forces inherent in all.

We begin with the motherline because the mother is the first ancestor we unconsciously know. Many of us have complications in our relationship with our mothers, and so motherline work can be particularly challenging and/or healing as we confront what may be a barrier to further seeking. I once led a group in a variation of the meditation I present in this chapter, and a participant skipped her own mother as an ancestor before realizing what she'd done. Sometimes our disconnection begins at home, and that is where our reconnection must begin, too. Motherline work can expand our concept of *mother* for ourselves and future generations, freeing us from the confines of cultural stories around mothers and mothering.

The motherline is also our unifier. Ancestor work is rooted in simultaneity: linear time becomes cyclic, duality becomes both/and, the diverse and specific ancestry of the individual is both apart from and a part of the collective. While we all have different mothers, every human ever born on this earth was cradled in the womb of a mother.

The womb is our common ancestor. We must remember.

The Dísir and the Protective Circle

In my spiritual tradition, which is based in the pre-Christian traditions of Northern Europe, the female ancestors or motherline spirits are attached to a lineage. They are the protectors, nurturers of future generations, guardians of the ørlög, or fate, of each generation, influencers of the weaving of wyrd, or destiny.

Ørlög and wyrd are sometimes seen as interchangeable terms, ørlög from Old Norse and wyrd from Old Anglo Saxon, though Urð in Old Norse is linguistically connected to wyrd. I see them as similar terms, but different in form, and I recommend Dr. Jenny Blain's wonderful essay *Approaching Wyrd* for a more in-depth exploration on this distinction. For the purposes of our journey, ørlög is the ancient primordial law, the warp of the universe on the loom of the Norns, the ancient mothers, the triple goddesses who emerged at the beginning of time and who sit at the base of the World Tree Yggdrasil weaving and carving the world in the web of wyrd. Wyrd is woven weft on the warp of ørlög, the pattern of our lives and the universe influenced by our actions.

Our ancestors shaped our ørlög and have a vested interest in the weaving of our wyrd. The female ancestors in my tradition are called the Dísir, plural of the word Dís, which means "Sister, Female Guardian . . . Goddess."[4] They were propitiated regularly with thanks offerings, called on to attend women in childbirth. They had an annual feast, the Dísablót, which was celebrated at different times, one being in late autumn, another being at midwinter.

In the Northern Hemisphere, where I now write, we are in the liminal space of the Dísir, the time where the realms of seen and unseen are less separate, where we can open to communication from our sacred grandmothers.

Runes as Ancestors

Our ancestors can help to teach us about the runes, but I have also found it helpful to think of the runes *as* ancestors. In many ways they literally are: rune inscriptions hold information from our ancient past and speak to our unconscious mind in a language that is deeply ancestral. Many people write to me saying they "know" or "recognize" the runes—something is being communicated by the presence of the shapes themselves. As wyrd, in the universal web of connection runes vibrate along the strands of our becoming. In this way they connect us both forward and back through time, to our ancestral past and our descendants to be.

The following practices are useful in creating sacred space for your rune practice and aligning it with ancestor work. They are usually mutually supportive.

Creation of an Ancestor Altar

An altar is a place of offering and focus. The roots of the word *altar* come from "burning" and "high"—lifted up—related to burnt offerings. Altars have different meanings in different traditions, so what do altars look like in the spiritual traditions of your lineage or lineages? The desire in research is not to replicate, but to allow for the information and historical context of altar work to flood your psyche—the realm of ancestral memory.

In creating your own ancestor altar, invoke your intuition and begin by feeling into what your ancestors would wish for this focus point in your practice. Altars may be indoors or outdoors; they may be simple or complex. Altars may change as your practice changes and new information emerges. They may include photos, symbols, natural elements, food, drink, flowers, or could be only a list of names, a prayer and a candle or glass of water.

Creating a ritual that can be done daily around your altar gives a muscle memory and focus to your psyche. I write with my ancestors or divinities every morning, lighting a candle and writing to them in letter form, then pausing and breathing, allowing them to write me back. When the ritual is done, I blow out the candle, closing the energy. A ritual can be simply sitting with your ancestors or leaving an offering on your altar.

Once daily is the initial intention behind this practice, but a small ritual done morning and night can give structure to your days and dreamtime and increase your ancestral awareness.

Our ancestors wish to be remembered. This is our primary offering at the altar: our attention, our curiosity, or willingness to show up, and our gratitude.

Under the Cloak

Another ritual practice from my spiritual tradition is adapted here to aid in sensory deepening and meditation.

The territory of the ancestors is the unseen. Sometimes by removing our sense of sight we can travel more quickly and with greater ease into the realm of dreams, visions, the unconscious, symbolic, spiritual.

For this exercise, prepare for meditation by draping a shawl or scarf over your head and shoulders when meditating with the intent of ancestral connection. Be sure to leave breathing room, and use a fabric wide or dense enough to block out most light. The most effective way to use this exercise is in a dark room or at night, but I tire easily so have found daytime meditation more fruitful.

You may use this technique with the meditation below or with any other practice that helps you get rooted—breathing deeply, humming or toning, listening to your heart.

The Grandmothers Meditation

This exercise creates a sacred circle of protection around you and engages in the imaginal as you begin this journey into your lineage.

This meditation can be used with any of the three variations, or you can modify it with your own.

Begin to breathe deeply and imagine you are a great tree with roots reaching down into the earth. Start to draw energy up through your roots; you can imagine it as liquid or light. Feel the energy reach the bottom of your feet and begin to fill your body. It rises up through your legs, through your pelvis and belly, up the curve of your spine, opening your heart, up your arms and throat, through your face and head, emerging from the crown of your head as branches. Breathe the energy up wide through your branches, until they become heavy and dip down again to the earth. Breathe in this way, a circuit. Root and ground.

From here imagine yourself on a vast beach. The air is warm, the wind light, the sky dark. No moon.

Down the beach you see a glow. You begin to walk toward the glow and notice an opening in the sand filled with warm, potent light. There is a ladder into the opening, which extends down toward the glow, and you begin to climb down the ladder rung by rung, until you are in a vast cavern. Feel the warmth and safety of this ancient place, glowing and easy. You notice some women coming toward you. These are your most recent ancestors—maybe you knew them; maybe they are recently departed; maybe you have seen them in photos; maybe they have been gone a long while. They greet you with love, surround you in the circle of their love. Notice what they do, what they wear, their countenance. Greet them as you would in life.

Then you see more women behind them. These are the ancestors of the preceding generation. They greet you with love, surround you in the circle of their love. Notice what they do, what they wear, their countenance. Greet them as you would in life.

You see more women behind them. These are the ancestors of the last century.

They greet you with love, surround you in the circle of their love. Notice what they do, what they wear, their countenance. Greet them as you would in life.

The cavern is expanding as more women join the circle around you, their beloved child and descendant. These are the ancestors of three hundred years past. They greet you with love, surround you in the circle of their love. Notice what they do, what they wear, their countenance. Greet them as you would in life.

More women join the circle. These are the ancestors from the past thousand years.

They greet you with love, surround you in the circle of their love. Notice what they do, what they wear, their countenance. Greet them as you would in life.

More women join the circle. These are the ancestors from the past two thousand years. They greet you with love, surround you in the circle of their love. Notice what they do, what they wear, their countenance. Greet them as you would in life.

More women join the circle, the cavern expands again. These are the ancestors from the past six thousand years. They greet you with love, surround you in the circle of their love. Notice what they do, what they wear, their countenance. Greet them as you would in life.

Already you are surrounded by millions of ancestral grandmothers. Feel that holding, the power of this, your lineage. Were we to travel back further, you would have billions. You are welcome to continue this visioning back through the matrix of time. Mitochondrial Eve, the lineage mother ancestor of all living humans, lived approximately 200,000 years ago.

Rest in this circle. Feel their gratitude. Offer yours in return. Ask a question if you like.

(Variation 2: Make your ancestral grandmothers an offering. Variation 3: Receive a sacred gift from one of your grandmothers.)

Now it is time to return.

The circle begins to dissipate as the women of your lineage leave the cavern. At last you are left with your known female ancestors. Bid them goodbye for now, but know you can always call on them, always return to this circle, anytime you need support or protection, anytime you wish to offer and share from your life.

As the last ancestor leaves, you walk to the ladder and climb up, rung by rung, wholly at peace and deeply nourished. You stand again on the beach and begin to breathe the energy back into your body from the earth below, the sky above. Bring your awareness into your physical being, wiggle your fingers and toes, and before you open your eyes, seal this time with a blessing.

This meditation can be repeated in an endless number of variations. If you don't like the cave as a metaphor, you can use natural formations of your choosing.

Trust the guidance that comes to you through the meeting of your sacred grandmothers. If in any of this ancestral work you feel uncertain, call on your lineage keepers to help with discernment.

We are never alone. I hope you can feel how truly held you are.

YOUR RUNE PRACTICE

A Guide to the Weekly Work

The Rune Poems

As we connect with our ancestors, we can also begin to craft our rune practice, drawing from the wisdom of ancient written resources. It is helpful to remember that the pre-Christian traditions of Northern Europe were oral traditions, and the surviving information—often preserved in manuscripts by classically trained Christian monks, who added their own interpretation to the record—is deeply fragmented. The Anglo-Saxon, Icelandic, and Norwegian rune poems are the only surviving written materials with the potential to carry the meanings of the runes. I say *potential*, because we don't actually know the function of these poems and can only guess that they carry significance. The runes are also mentioned in primary texts, such as the Sagas and Eddas, and found as either pre-runic writing or later inscriptions on a wide variety of archaeological materials, from runestones to combs to shields, but they are not listed by name nor explained with any meaning attached.

In a riddle befitting the *kennings* or associative poems in the runic literature, the oldest rune poem is also the newest. It is from England, written in Old Anglo-Saxon, and contains information on twenty-six runes. The poem's original manuscript—believed to be from the eighth or ninth century CE and preserved in a tenth-century document[5]—was destroyed in a fire in 1731.[6] The manuscript that has survived is a copy created by George Hickes in 1703,[7] and many scholars question the authenticity of this edition's transcription and interpretation. It is impossible to know what was in the original manuscript or how true the later edition compares, but the similarities between this rune poem and the others are enough to offer the possibility of authenticity.

There are also rune poems from Iceland, written in Old Icelandic sometime in the fifteenth century, which have content similar to the Norwegian rune poem, written in Old Norse in the thirteenth century and preserved in a manuscript which was later destroyed.[8] All that survives are the transcriptions, and like the Anglo-Saxon rune poem, those are the source of many academic questions.

All rune poems carry lore in allegory and riddle, packets of metaphorical language. For each week's study I include rune poems for you to explore in several forms: the original poems in Old Icelandic, Old Norwegian, and Old Anglo-Saxon; a widely used translation of the poem in English from the nineteenth-century book *Runic and Heroic Poems of the Old Teutonic Peoples* by Bruce Dickins, which has impacted what people say the rune "means" in contemporary time; and my own translation of the rune poems.

Translation as a Spiritual Practice

I am not a translator.

I am a curious former academic with a brain injury, so it was surprising to find myself translating the rune poems for this book. I'd never attempted any sort of translation before, with the exception of required assignments for high school French and college Spanish classes. In spite of my brief experiences with Romance languages, my linguistic fluency is in English, and I've never studied anything else. The pull to translation began in my rune practice when I felt called to look up words and get my own sense of what the rune poems were saying. It began as a hunch. Many of the words in contemporary English have evolved from Old Anglo-Saxon, which shares a Proto-Germanic root with Icelandic and Norwegian. I started to feel like the nineteenth-century translations of the rune poems weren't giving me the whole story, and I began dreaming of the languages of my ancestors. My first attempt was with the rune poem for IOR. Since beginning this journey, the experience has been profound.

We don't know what the runes mean. There is no definitive source that spells it out clearly. We are missing the historical context of the runes, the culture and society from which they came. Our source materials have been mostly rewritten and translated. Those translators—even those with a deep understanding of ancient grammar and culture—still rely on inference and, like so much in translation, judgment. In translation a word may have many meanings, so a translator makes a judgment based sometimes on deep knowledge but other times for poetic purpose or personal interpretation. When we read a translation, especially of an ancient primary source in a language no longer spoken—like Old Anglo-Saxon—we are reading such an interpretation.

A huge part of my spiritual path has been coming into my own gnosis, my own interpretation, claiming my willingness to be wrong in the service of opening dialogue and believing that we all can access spiritual information. Rather than just relying on others to interpret the rune poems, discovering my way through the meanings has helped deepen and transform my relationship with the runes.

My translations are inexact and not grammatically accurate. Without a base knowledge of grammar, I am simply looking words up in dictionaries or finding root words and making connections. I am okay with being incorrect in substance, but correct in feeling—the important aspect of this practice is developing relationship. When we release ourselves from the rote, standardized "knowing" so common in contemporary culture, we come closer to our ancestors lived experiences. For example, most of the poems are gendered masculine, although the word *man* in Old Anglo-Saxon can mean man or woman, so I might experiment with gender in the synthesis of partnership. Some words did not appear in the dictionary at all, and I have indicated where that happened.

It is hard for me to put such material out there because it is so imperfect, but the imperfection is actually the point: You too can discover the meaning of the rune poems for yourself. You too can begin to decode these languages and feel into the interpretations that are authentic to you.

The ancestors whisper, constantly: *There is no one way, there is only the way.*

I learned a lot in the process, and I feel like my later translation attempts were stronger than my first. I resisted the urge to go through and correct all of my previous translations, because as with my other books, I feel that showing the process can sometimes support another's journey.

I don't offer my translations for you to use as meaning. I offer them with the hope my messy attempts will inspire you to engage your own wisdom, to explore these ancient languages in a spiritual practice.

What I've found in the work of translation is exhilarating: a curious freedom in not relying on the usual, a magic in translating a word with varied meaning. For example in the FEHU Anglo-Saxon rune poem, a word normally translated as "lord" or "king," *drihtne*, also means "dead body" or "cadaver." This gives an entirely new feel to the poem and, for me, to the meaning of the rune.

It is refreshing to remember that we can access this information for ourselves and come into a direct context with the words and ways of our ancestors through the study of their language roots and myths. There is no wrong way to explore this work. Those who translated before us were not contemporaries of the rune poem authors, and their work is interpretive, too. When we move past the idea of being right or wrong, we can move into a realm of spiritual intuition, which aligns with ancestral earth ways as recorded in ancient texts.

It is also important to recall, again, that, like all Northern European sacred texts, these were transcribed from a more ancient oral tradition. Not all runes have rune poems, not all poems complement each other. In a both-and universe, we explore what is and what remains.

I offer resources at the end of this book for those who wish to pursue their own translations.

Inquiry Practice

For each week I offer a set of questions to ask the rune being you are working with. These are only a starting place: Your questions through this week—the ones that arise gently from your curiosity and the relationships you build—will always be more beautiful than any I craft externally, and I hope you will listen for those queries. I also understand, however, that we sometimes need a jumping-off point for our own imaginings, so you can think of the weekly questions as that space of opening that we step through in any door.

When I exchange inquiry with a being or deity, I tend to use the epistolary or letter writing format. I write to the being and then freehand as the being writes back. This is part of my daily ritual writing practice and not for everyone, but I do encourage you to find a communication practice that works for you.

Notice the cyclic nature and overlap in this conversation. You will see this both through the book and the course of our practice, a rhythm of repetition.

Part of this is due to my disability: I have neuro-inflammation that causes memory issues, so I tend to repeat myself. But I have learned to embrace it as a method of psychological and spiritual recognition. When you notice something repeating, pay attention. It means your subconscious has acknowledged it as important.

Galdr and Toning the Runes

Galdr is a word that means "magic song, charm" in Old Icelandic. It also appears in Old Anglo-Saxon, where it is defined as "incantation, divination, enchantment, a charm, magic, sorcery." The words appear in medieval manuscripts like Nigon Wyrta Galdor or Nine Herbs Charm in the *Lacnunga* as methods for singing healing into a spell by invoking the qualities and personalities of plants used and in the Poetic Edda and several sagas as a means for magic.

The runes are more than shapes; they are also sounds. In your weekly practice with each rune you may wish to begin chanting or singing the name of the rune as another path to connection. So much of our ancestral legacy was once oral, communicated exclusively through sound rather than through writing. I find that toning the runes in a rhythm helps me attune to other aspects of their presence.

You might begin toning a rune in front of your altar or as a periodic practice over the course of each day as you work through your week with the rune. I like to tone the runes as I draw them, when I am making a rune set, or to make an offering of my energy during meditation. Sound—breath, voice, vibration—is another means for personal connection.

Suggested Structure for Weekly Practice

This structure is meant as a scaffold for your engagement. As time goes on you will likely feel called to change the rhythm and format—and that is a good thing. It means the practice is becoming your own. But to begin, here's what has worked best for my circles in the Live Gnosis Group:

To begin your week set your rune altar with a physical representation of the rune you are working with, some sort of visual so you can see the rune as you move through your days. Sometimes I use my own illustrations or the runes from my set, but I have also found natural objects like sticks or plants in the shape of the runes work well too. Plan to visit your altar space daily in a ritual practice—lighting a candle, singing, meditation with the rune.

Also at the beginning of your week start your rune inquiry. In the first days with the rune spend some time asking questions. These can be formal/journaled as suggested or held peripherally in mind as you move through the day. See what answers come in your waking life and in your dream space. Write down any impressions you might have.

Invite the rune through sacred art practice. Spend some time drawing the rune—the shape of it on its own or in conjunction, like the rune twirls—to get a sense of how it appears.

Tone the rune with galdr at your altar or as you work with the rune in other ways. See how the song changes throughout the week.

Craft meditation journeys with the rune, using the Grandmother's Meditation as a template to descend and visit the essence of the rune as an ancestor.

Midway through your week start to look at the rune poems both in the old languages and in translation. See if there are any words that stand out to you and consider looking them up. Start to find the intersections between your rune inquiry, art, galdr, notes, and the rune poems.

As you conclude each week with the rune, consider making a ritual of thanks offering and closing, maybe giving the rune some food or drink and letting the rune know you are changing your focus but that you intend to keep working in relationship.

Ultimately, this is your process. As you continue in relationship you will find some aspects of the practice are affirming and others less so. The energy of adaptation is part of relationship, so trust the path and allow yourself to find what works best for you.

A note on repetition: I have neuro-inflammation and tend to repeat myself. There will be repetitions in this work, in this book, which are consistent with my experience of mythic, ancestral time. One of the ways I have been able to embrace my disability as part of my spiritual path is to see repetitions as messages to pay attention—this is important. You are invited into the experience of rhythm and difference, a pattern made beautiful in its emphasis.

Making Your Rune Set

Developing an intimacy with the runes over this practice may involve making your own rune set. Runes can be made from many substances, including wood, stone, clay, cloth, paper—anything really. Some ancient literature exists to support making runes from wood pieces cut from a nut or fruit-bearing tree, carved and stained red. But the purpose of this journey is gnosis work with the runes, and for this we will need to both understand lore *and* follow our inner impulses.

When I first began studying the runes, I crafted a set from a single branch of a hazel tree, cut by hand, carved by hand, and stained with blood. Once a month I would paint the runes with my menstrual blood, chanting their names and then singing a blessing over them as they dried. These deeply personal devotional rites were private, as was this rune set.

No one told me how to make a set of runes. I asked the runes how they wanted to be made, then followed my intuition. One branch of a hazel tree I had blessed and with which I had interacted within ritual suddenly died and was the perfect diameter for a rune set. I had had a deep relationship with hazel for years, performing daily rituals in a hazel grove during a time of difficult transition. The tree spirits knew and recognized me. The branch was an offering.

I knew also for this particular set I needed to cut the branch by hand. My children, then twelve and ten, held the branch while I sawed it with a dull pruner, sweating and reveling in the physicality of the work. I sanded the cut rounds. Then, with a rudimentary set of carving tools, I etched each rune.

The blood offering was also instinctive. I knew some runestones in Scandinavia showed evidence of staining with ocher. I had worked with women's mysteries for five years at that point and felt my blood charged with power.

When I painted the runes, they came alive to me, as if the form of them were recognizing my DNA. Intuitively, I fed them monthly. Intuitively, I sang.

I did find text later to support my intuition, explorations with the runes that connect them with feminine mysteries and magic.

But here's the thing about this wyrd traveling: it is not rooted in text. You are welcome to explore text and invited to read and develop your own ideas about the runes, but the baseline of the Wild Soul Rune Path is relationship.

If you choose to make a set of runes through this experience, consider asking the runes how they would like to be made.

If you are coming to the runes from an ancestral perspective, consider asking your ancestors how they worked with the runes.

If you are coming to the runes out of a recognition of shape or tone, consider feeling into their shapes and tones as you dream of making.

Above all, trust your process and engage with these ancient beings in reverence and respect.

Before we begin the practice, I would like to invite you on a journey through the wyrd. It is my own path, wending and incomplete, but in it I have found great alignment with the primary texts and lore of the runes. It is the basis for this journey and method of relationship building and begins in lineage like all things of mythic significance in the web of origin.

The Feminine Origins of the Runes: Myth and Lore

My mother has a pendant inscribed in runes from her father's hometown of Bergen, Norway. On one side it bears an engraving of a spinning wheel, on the other mysterious writing that captivated me as a child. In early college I paid a student of languages to translate the pendant for me. It was written not in new Norwegian, but in Old Norse and read, "Lake, River, Mountain, Norway." I thought the words lovely, if pedestrian. I didn't know that each letter was also a rune, each symbol more than a word, but rather a "secret or whispered mystery."[9] It would be nearly two decades before the runes would come into my life as beings and creatures that sing songs and inform.

Modern scholars have puzzled over the origins of the runes. There is a conflict in the interpretation of the runes, for they are seen as either a pragmatic alphabet or a magical, ritual tool.[10] Logical conclusions run that runes were both. Professor Adrian Poruciuc writes, "Much of the mystery that surrounds runes is actually due to the failure of practically all attempts at establishing where, when and by whom runes were 'invented.'"[11]

Amid such flummoxing resistance to a developmental timeline, archaeological evidence appears to be equally obscure. The generally accepted oldest datable—and, I would say, translatable—runic inscription on an archaeological object is on the Vimose comb from 160 CE Denmark,[12] which appears to bear the name of its owner. And an earlier find—the Meldorf fibula, from 50 CE in North Germany—is possibly a runic inscription . . . or proto-runic . . . or Roman;[13] the arguments prevail in the absence of evidence.

In looking for the origins of the runes, I turn then to mythology for a clue of where to pick up a trail deep and historically cold. In the *Hávamál*, a poem from the Elder Poetic Edda recorded in thirteenth-century Iceland, the runes are attributed to a "taking" by the god Oðin after sacrifice:

I ween that I hung | on the windy tree,
   Hung there for nights full nine;
   With the spear I was wounded, | and offered I was
   To Othin, myself to myself,
   On the tree that none | may ever know
   What root beneath it runs.
None made me happy | with loaf or horn,
   And there below I looked;
   I took up the runes, | shrieking I took them,
   And forthwith back I fell[14]

And this is where the story begins to turn on itself, becoming a cycle in mythic time, an exercise in simultaneity rather than linearity. For the *Hávamál* poem is known as "The Words of the High One,"[15] and that high one is Oðin, the All Father, the sacrificial god. Where he takes the runes *from* may speak to their origins more fully than any allowable evidence and may afford a continuity, a connection between the sacred symbols of past civilizations.

I would argue that the origins of the runes are neither linguistic nor exclusively mythic, but rather sacred feminine magic, held in the trust-memory of prehistoric, Old European civilizations. Their origins and functions have been long obscured, but they transitioned into our history through myths reflecting conflict, masculine-feminine partnership, and healing. But in order to parallel the runes with both magic and the feminine, there is another aspect of the tale. This is where I find the runes in my own life, again.

Runic Mysteries and Skara Brae

I may have arrived faster to the runes had I been braver. In 1998, I traveled to Europe alone, a pilgrimage to the home of my dead grandfather, Sigurd Rosenlund, in Norway. I was supposed to arrive in London, then take a bus tour through England and Scotland, ending in the Orkney Islands where there is a ferry direct to Bergen. But at the last minute I canceled. It was my first time traveling alone. I was twenty-three. I was afraid.

Fast-forward through linear time: In 2013, I began taking classes with a community of rune seekers practicing in-depth gnosis work. I developed a powerful relationship with the runes, seeing them as individual beings, in the same way that each letter is both a symbol and a sound, each rune is the keeper of information.

Last year an art commission drew me to the Orkney Islands again, and it is there I found in Skara Brae the evidence I sought, linking the runes to a deeper history than the Vikings or the Eddas, the comb or the fibula. Skara Brae is a Neolithic settlement in the Orkney Islands inhabited from 3200 to 2200 BCE.[16] This time frame falls partially within the Old European period defined by archaeologist Dr. Marija Gimbutas as an era from "the 7th to the 3rd millennia BC . . . referring to Neolithic Europe before the Indo Europeans."[17] Orkney falls outside of the Old European geographical area, which is typically viewed as southern continental Europe. What drew my attention to this particular complex was the presence of "pre-runic" writing. As I looked closely at the symbols carved at Skara Brae I recognized not just "pre-runic" markings, but runes.

I had the same feeling of revelation when I saw the diagram of Old European script from Gimbutas's book, *Civilizations of the Goddess*. Embedded in the ancient symbolic language of Old Europe are the distinct shapes of multiple runes, as well as numerous markings that parallel those at Skara Brae.

In his article "Old European Echoes in Germanic Runes?" Dr. Adrian Poruciuc explores the parallels between the runes and the symbol systems of Old Europe but resists the linearity/logical theory of development for the runic symbolic alphabet. "Runologists should give up striving to discover a single origin for the Germanic runic script and to view that script as only alphabetic."[18] He cites the use of runes for divination as part of a broader symbolic understanding rooted in a magical or sacred context and paralleling many of the rune signs with the Old European script.[19]

When I view the ancient script of Old Europe beside the pre-runic symbols of Skara Brae, something stirs in my cells. There is a story here—a story the stone carvings carry.

One further artifact from the Orkney Islands is worth mentioning as we proceed with the next phase of our journey. This is from the excavation at the Links of Noltland: a tiny human-shaped figurine, some 5,000 years old, her body marked with circles for breasts and a deep *V* between them. They call her the Orkney Venus.[20] She is the oldest Neolithic human figure discovered thus far in Northern Europe. And she is distinctly female.

The Runes and the Goddess

If the runes are a magical symbol system from Old European culture, then we must turn to the stories, the myths—for these tales contain sacred symbols and these too can help us to create a fuller view of lost or obscured worlds. In looking to the myths, I ask: What is the relationship of the feminine to magic in the ancient Northern European spiritual traditions? Is there evidence in the myths to support a transitional relationship between the pre-Indo European cultures of Northern Europe and the cultures of pre-Indo European Old Europe? To attempt an understanding we turn to explore the ancient threads of the feminine through textual mythology, particularly looking at the stories of the Æsir-Vanir War, the Völva, the Norns, and Gullveig to try to establish the origins of the runes and their relationship to the feminine. I begin with the storyteller, the potent memory of female magic in ancient Northern European culture.

The Völva

In the *Voluspá* poem from the Poetic Edda, Oðin calls forth a Völva—a witch or seer—from her grave. According to scholar Max Dashú, founder of the Suppressed Histories archive, the word *völva* comes from *valr*, "The Norse name for a ritual staff, *valr*, gave rise to *völva* and *vala*, names for female shamans."[21] The Völva of the *Völuspá* poem is ancient, of the race of giants or Jotun, old enough to remember the beginning of the world, the history of all the nine worlds, and all the races.

> *I remember yet the giants of beginning*
> *Who fed me in the days gone by*
> *Nine women I home, nine giantesses*
> *Measuring-tree glorious before mold from beneath.*

That the Völva comes from an ancient people that existed prior to Oðin's community of gods, the Æsir, is significant in our search for runic origins, as is the practice of seiðr, or shamanic magic, both by Oðin and the Völva in the *Völuspá*. In the *Ynglinga Saga* it is written, "Njord's daughter Freyja was priestess of the sacrifices (seiðr), and first taught the Asaland people the magic art, as it was in use and fashion among the Vanaland people."[22] In an interesting twist, if Freyja is practiced in the magic arts, she may be a descendant of the Völva Oðin wakes by the very necromancy Freyja teaches him.

The goddess Freyja is one of the Vanir, a race of gods whose name may etymologically be rooted in words meaning "friend," "pleasure," or "desire," and who are often associated with fertility, divination, and magic.[23] Oðin is one of the Æsir, a word of questionable origin and at the center of a debate about who the elder gods in the Norse pantheon are. Snorri Sturluson, purported scribe of the Sagas and Prose Edda in the thirteenth century, cites the origin of the word *Æsir* as Ásía, "the Old Norse word for Asia,"[24] which has its uses in the discussion to follow, though it is much debated.

The Æsir are referred to as the high gods, or sky gods, and occupy a different realm in the Nine Worlds than the Vanir. The war between the Æsir and the Vanir is described in the *Völuspá* by the Völva: "She remembers the first war in the world."[25] That the ancient seeress from the race of giants would remember the first of all wars is not in itself significant, but the fact that war did not always exist but had a "first" and her memory of the cause of the war are incredibly important. This brings us to Gullveig, source of the first war and feminine magic.

She remembered great battle, the first in the world
That Gullveig spears pierced
And in the High One's hall he burned her
Thrice burned, Thrice born
Often, repeatedly, still she lives.

Heið they call her, wheresoever to houses she came
Wise Woman Witch crafting prophecy, knowledge her magic staff
She made enchantment wheresoever she knew, working a spell she
  entranced
Always beloved, she was sweet odor to ill women.

The source of the Æsir-Vanir war was the abuse and burning of the Vanir goddess Gullveig, whose name means "gold" (*gull*) "drink" or "strength" (*veig*).[26] The symbolism of gold in Northern Europe "is obviously associated (in Old Norse poetry) with divine brightness, illumination within darkness, great cosmic forces and hidden wisdom."[27] Gullveig is stabbed with spears and three times burned, yet she emerges reborn three times as well—as a different goddess with a different name of Heið. Heið is a common name for seeresses and giants in the Sagas. In Old Icelandic, the word means "bright (clear) sky."[28]

The result of Gullveig's initiation through death and rebirth is the creation of a powerful feminine presence: Heið, the seeress, the practitioner of seiðr magic. She is associated with magic wands or staffs, prophecy, and trance, and her relationship with women is established in the final line of the stanza, as she "was a sweet odor to ill women."

The word *illrar* is often translated as "evil" relative to women in the *Völuspá*. I choose to translate it as "ill," like Maria Kvilhaug, who states, "The Norse word is *illrar*, which means bad, or wicked, and is the origin of the English word 'ill', 'sick'. I have always suspected the original meaning to be 'sick women', because there are several Norse references to how the goddesses and witches may help sick women . . . Of course, 'bad' can be just another word for unconventional."[29] She also reminds us that the writers of the Eddas were believed to be Christian monks, to whom all feminine magic must be necessarily evil. Of a similar mind, other scholars translate the word as "contrary."[30]

Gullveig's transformation is remarkable for its endurance, bringing to mind the transformative initiations of the Eleusinian Mysteries in ancient Greece, incorporating the potent magic of death and rebirth into a new cosmic order. That her treatment inspires war between the Æsir and the Vanir is seen by many scholars as reflective of invasion patterns, similar to those described by Gimbutas's Kurgan Theory. "Since the Vanir are fertility deities, the war has often been understood as the reflection of the overrunning of local fertility cults somewhere in the Germanic area by a more warlike cult, perhaps that of invading Indo-Europeans."[31] The war ends in peace and reconciliation. From the sacrifice and initiation of Gullveig/Heið emerges a specific form of women's magic known to the Vanir goddess Freyja. After the peace of the Æsir and the Vanir, which may provide evidence of a partnership between divergent spiritual cosmologies, Freyja moves to the Æsir realm of Asgard and shares seiðr with Oðin. For this reason, Gullveig/Heið is often seen as an aspect of the goddess Freyja, though I resist this merging due to a personal desire to keep the old stories and goddesses complex, rather than simplifying them.

And it is in the spirit of this complexity that I introduce the Norns who have a role both in women's magic and in the origins of the runes.

The Norns

Ash know I stands, is called Ygg's horse (Yggdrasil)
High tree, sprinkled with white wet sand;
From there come dews those in dales fall;
Stands ever green over the well of Fate (Urð).

Then come maidens many knowing
Three out of the hall that under tree stands
Fate (Urð) is called one, another To Happen (Verðandi)
They cut in wood—Debt (Skuld) is third.
They laws laid, they lives chose.
Lifetimes children, fate to tell.

The Norns are mystery figures in Norse myth. They seem to function in multiple ways, primarily as the keepers of fate or wyrd both as individual spirits (plural: Nornir) and as a sort of Triple Goddess creatrix at the base of the World Tree. In the *Völuspá* translation above, the Norns emerge from the well of Urð at the base of the World Tree, a well defined as "wyrd or fate."[32] Urð is the name of one of the three Norns listed in the passage, as well as Verðandi, from the root *verða*, "to happen, come to pass,"[33] and Skuld, "debt,"[34] as in, the future is indebted to the past. The Norns are a personification of mythic time, a cycle or spiral that is the many and the all: everything that was, everything that is, everything that will be. They are nonlinear and simultaneous, like myth itself.

The Norns' relationship with mythic time is potentially significant in the search for the runic connections with the divine feminine. They are from the well of origin, and simultaneously are origin itself. They are often seen as weavers, winding the thread of wyrd for individual and cosmic fate. Their number three parallels an earlier mention in the *Völuspá* regarding three maidens emerging from Jotunheim, the land of giants:

In their dwellings at peace | they played at tables,
Of gold no lack | did the gods then know,—
Till thither came | up giant-maids three,
Huge of might, | out of Jotunheim.[35]

The connection of the Norns to the giants—thus kin to the Völva—is important. The Jotun are considered the primeval race in the Nine Worlds, those who were present at the beginning of historical time, but they are actually prehistoric and thus pre-temporal at least in a linear sense. It makes sense that they would be the keepers of destiny, in the same way the Völva is the keeper of oral history. They transcend the new Gods, both the Æsir and the Vanir, and yet are in a complex series of relationships with them for all of time.

Let's revisit the *Hávamál*, where Oðin details his sacrifice and acquisition of the runes:

> And there below I looked;
> I took up the runes, | shrieking I took them,
> And forthwith back I fell.

Oðin is seen as hanging himself from the World Tree, over the Well of Urð, taking and grasping the runes from the well. The word used to describe Oðin's action in Old Norse is *nám*, a word with a variety of meanings including both "to take," as in "take possession of," and "to perceive or learn."[36] The well of the Nornir is the source of their origin, the source of nourishment for the World Tree, and the source of the web of wyrd or fate. This would imply that the runes are a part of these things: origin, nourishment of all life, the wyrd, the Nornir themselves. Did Oðin take the runes without the Nornir's permission? Or is this a tale of partnership, of sacrifice and exchange?

And so the story stretches.

In the *Völuspá* Oðin, as one of the Æsir, participates in the forced initiation of Gullveig/Heið and sees her receive the power of seiðr through her ordeal. In the *Hávamál*, Oðin experiences his own willing initiation—his hanging, his sacrifice—but instead of receiving the power of divine illumination like Gullveig/Heið, his sacrifice is not self-contained. When he takes up the runes, they come from somewhere. In the same way he had to learn seiðr from Freyja, Oðin needed to take the runes from the well of the Nornir. Perhaps enacting an ancient ritual of sacrificial exchange, Oðin paid the price for a wisdom either taken or learned, sourced from the feminine well of origin.

Based on the mythology of the Poetic Edda, the roots of magic in Northern European pre-Christian traditions appears to be feminine. The origin of the Völva extends back to the race of giants, to the beginning of time, suggesting that the magical and prophetic abilities of women—at least those of Jotun blood—are innate, primary. The removal of the runes from the well of the

Nornir posits an origin to the runes from a time before the gods. That Oðin has to learn or take magical tools and abilities from women may serve as a metaphor for a transition in Northern Europe from women's power to male power or a deep understanding of necessary, less binary partnership.

This isn't to say that magic and the runes are the exclusive dominion of women. It is, however, to imply that the powers of women in early Northern European cultures were significant and important in relationship to the community as a whole. In looking at the forms of the runes relative to other Old European script symbols, it would seem there could be a common root. And within Old European cultures there was a powerful reverence for the Goddess and the potency of women as life-givers and connectors to divinity. Northern Europe had a divine cosmology that illustrates in myth an initial clash between two "races" of divinities, but the Vanir did not convert to the religion of the invader—presuming the Æsir *did* represent an invading force of new gods. Instead they made peace, exchanged wisdom, intermarried, and cocreated new stories together.

Women in Northern Europe were famously free during the Viking era, able to fight, hold property, divorce, and rule in ways women elsewhere were not. The Oseberg ship burial, one of the most resplendent archaeological finds of the Viking age, is dated to 834 CE and contains the remains of two women with distaffs.[37] That these women were Völvas seems a distinct possibility. Educator Kari Tauring says that, "Archeologists in Scandinavia have discovered wands (staffs) in about 40 female graves, usually rich graves with valuable grave offerings showing that Völvas belonged to the highest level of society.[38] Tauring also indicates that tradition of the Völva extended into recorded history and the position of women as diviners and seers in the Germanic tribes was commented on by Julius Caesar and Tacitus.[39] Perhaps the merging of different cosmologies and the sharing of magic empowered women in Northern European societies and allowed them to retain power, even in the face of changing spiritual traditions, until a spiritual climate arrived that could not tolerate other beliefs or perceptions. I speak, of course, of Christianity.

Is it possible that the magic of the ancient sacred feminine powers and the runes hold keys for surviving patriarchy, healing from violence, and creating partner relationships?

If Gullvieg/Heið can transform through death and rebirth, allowing the magic of seiðr into the world and continuing to practice even after such terrifying torment, if Freyja can teach her former enemy the power of this deep, feminine magic even after such tremendous betrayal, if the Nornir in their wisdom can allow Oðin to take the runes from the well and share their whispered secrets with humankind, what lessons can we who have lived through thousands of years of burning, abuse, and theft by patriarchy and who have been both harmed and harmful in the structures of patriarchal power all learn in reestablishing partner relationships from the mysteries of the ancient past?

This question is poignant for me. I come to the magic of seiðr as a woman of multiple ancestries, as an American living on colonized land, far from my ancestral homes. I come to the runes as a mother of a son and of daughters and as a partner and protector of the powerful relationship between the masculine and feminine entities in us all. I come as a seeker of the ways of my ancestors, called to discover their fragments and etchings, called to listen between the lines of their tales. I come afraid, for I have been taught to fear this wisdom of the symbols of my heritage due to their corruption and misappropriation in recent history. And I come unafraid, for the deeper I travel the more I find that sings me home.

When we claim the runes as a source wisdom partnership, when we stretch the threads of wyrd back far enough, through prehistory and view their shapes, we claim our own pain and capacity for power, magic, and healing. As we step toward the fire, once again, we can remember that in death is transformation, rebirth, the greater mysteries.

In this story that is my story—that is your story, reader, as you participate too—like the Nornir, beyond the bounds of logical time and space, in the mythic cycle of creation, there is potential—a soul seed as rich as the one the Völva knows, from the beginning of time. In such a seed grows the World Tree. In such a story of the past grows our present and our future.

May it be blessed.

THE RUNES

As you set out on your weekly practice, consider resisting the urge to run to the rune poems for answers or interpretation. Instead, ritualize the opening of each week and view the illustrations and questions. Journal for a few days, sing with the runes, use them in art or see where you find them in nature. Then, toward the end of the week, explore the rune poems and see how they align with your inner knowing.

At the end of this practice you will find some of my own explorations, an opportunity for you to explore another's gnosis once you have begun your own relationship with the runes.

The Elder Futhark

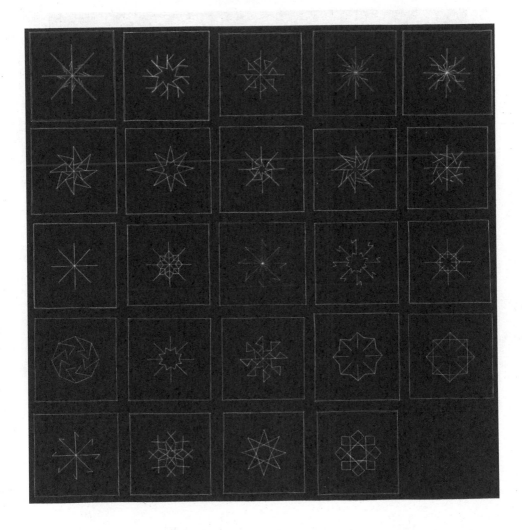

Week 1: FEHU

Inquiry for FEHU

Where did you begin?
What is your true name?
Whom do you honor? Who honors you?
What symbols do you bear?
What is your standard?
Where on the earth can you be found?
How do you prefer to receive offerings?
What is your relationship to my life?
What is your mode of expression?
What time of year is best for you?
What stories do you choose?
What elements are representative of your qualities?
How can I be of service to you?
Where do we begin?

Anglo-Saxon Rune Poem

> Feoh byþ frofur fira gehwylcum;
> sceal ðeah manna gehwylc miclun hyt dælan
> gif he wile for drihtne domes hleotan.

Dickins Translation

> Wealth is a comfort to all men;
> yet must every man bestow it freely,
> if he wish to gain honour in the sight of the Lord.

My Translation

> Cattle shall be comfort to each living being
> Must yet they all greatness hides bestow
> Gift they pleasure by cadaver judge cast lots

Icelandic Rune Poem

> Fé er frænda róg
> ok flæðar viti

ok grafseiðs gata
aurum fylkir.

Dickins Translation

Wealth
source of discord among kinsmen
and fire of the sea
and path of the serpent.

My Translation

Cattle/sheep
Who kinsman slander
Both poisoned punishment
And grave enchantments path
Gold king

Norwegian Rune Poem

Fé vældr frænda róge; føðesk ulfr í skóge.

Dickins Translation

Wealth is a source of discord among kinsmen;
the wolf lives in the forest.

My Translation

Wealth wailing kinsman slander, father wolf in wood.

Week 2: URUZ

Inquiry for URUZ

What is the source of your power?
Where is the sound of your name?
What rivers flow to your rhythm?
What oceans capture your melody?
Where do you live in my blood?
How can I taste you?
What offerings should I make to you?
Where is your memory located?
Who carries your bones?
How can I repair the rift in knowing?
What is the shape of your sorrow?
What is the shape of your joy?
How many homes do you hold in your presence?
Where can I find the power of my own?

Anglo-Saxon Rune Poem

Ur byþ anmod ond oferhyrned,
felafrecne deor, feohteþ mid hornum
mære morstapa; þæt is modig wuht.

Dickins Translation

The aurochs is proud and has great horns;
it is a very savage beast and fights with its horns;
a great ranger of the moors, it is a creature of mettle.

My Translation

Aurochs inhabits steadfast courageous daring and has horns above;
Very fierce bold wild animal, fights with horns;
Boundary traverser of moors, it is a brave wight.

Icelandic Rune Poem

Úr er skýja grátr
ok skára þverrir

ok hirðis hatr.
umbre vísi

Dickins Translation

Shower
lamentation of the clouds
and ruin of the hay-harvest
and abomination of the shepherd.

My Translation

Drizzling rain is clouds weeping
And raked decrease
And shepherd hatred.
Change leader.

Norwegian Rune Poem

Úr er af illu járn; opt løypr ræinn á hjarne.

Dickins Translation

Dross comes from bad iron;
the reindeer often races over the frozen snow.

My Translation

Drizzling rain is of evil iron;
Often trails reindeer on hard frozen snow.

I can't find the word *ræinn* in any dictionary. The contemporary Icelandic word for reindeer is *Hreindýr*, which is close, so I am choosing to translate *ræinn* as such.

Week 3: THURISAZ

Inquiry for THURISAZ

What is the thorn?
Who are the giants?
What is the sensation of relationship between the giants and women?
Where is misfortune?
Where is strength?
What is the intersection between misfortune and strength?
What offerings can I bring?
How do you receive them?
When did you become more than protection?
What is the function of pain?
How does the thorn resolve anger?
Where do we begin again?

Anglo-Saxon Rune Poem

> *Ðorn byþ ðearle scearp; ðegna gehwylcum*
> *anfeng ys yfyl, ungemetum reþe*
> *manna gehwelcum, ðe him mid resteð.*

Dickins Translation

> *The thorn is exceedingly sharp,*
> *an evil thing for any knight to touch,*
> *uncommonly severe on all who sit among them.*

My Translation

> *Thorn inhabits harsh, violent, vigorous; scrapes and irritates;*
> *servant every*
> *defender storm evil, immensely righteous*
> *man each, them him with to rest.*

Icelandic Rune Poem

> *Þurs er kvenna kvöl*
> *ok kletta búi*
> *ok varðrúnar verr.*
> *Saturnus þengill.*

Dickins Translation

Giant
torture of women
and cliff-dweller
and husband of a giantess.

My Translation

Giant is women agony
And rock estate
And became secrets worse.
Saturn king.

Norwegian Rune Poem

Þurs vældr kvinna kvillu;
kátr værðr fár af illu.

Dickins Translation

Giant causes anguish to women;
misfortune makes few men cheerful.

My Translation

Giant wailing women problems;
Cheerful rest very short of evil.

Week 4: ANSUZ

Inquiry for ANSUZ

Who is the breath?
Where does the breath come from?
What is the animating force?
How does the life force flow?
What happened in the beginning?
Which divinities do you represent?
What offerings are appropriate for the mouth and the voice?
Where can we experience you?
How do you call a name?
What is the being you honor?
Why does your name take multiple shapes?
Where can the connection come?
Who is the source of the breath?

Anglo-Saxon Rune Poem

> Os byþ ordfruma ælere spræce,
> wisdomes wraþu ond witena frofur
> and eorla gehwam eadnys ond tohiht.

Dickins Translation

> Os
> The mouth is the source of all language,
> a pillar of wisdom and a comfort to wise men,
> a blessing and a joy to every knight.

My Translation

> Divinity inhabits source dealer speech.
> Wisdom help and one who knows consolation,
> And earl each happiness and hope.

Icelandic Rune Poem

> Óss er algingautr
> ok ásgarðs jöfurr,

ok valhallar vísi.
Jupiter oddviti.

Dickins Translation

Óss - God
Aged Gautr
and prince of Ásgardr
and lord of Vallhalla.

My Translation

River's mouth is made perfect bragging
And Asgard's king
And Valhalla's leader
Jupiter leader.

I could not find direct translation in the Concise Dictionary of Old Icelandic (CDOI) for the word *algingautr. Algera* means "to finish, make perfect." *Gauta/ gautan* means "to brag/bragging."

Norwegian Rune Poem

Óss er flæstra færða
fǫr; en skalpr er svœrða.

Dickins Translation

As
Estuary is the way of most journeys;
but a scabbard is of swords.

My Translation

River mouth most brings
Journey; and scalp is sword.

Week 5: RAIDO

Inquiry for RAIDO

Who is the rider and who is ridden?
Where is the horse and who is the steed?
What sacrifices must be made?
Where do you accept such offerings?
How does the shape relate to the gift?
Who takes the high road?
Who takes the low road?
What is riding to those who walk?
Where do you travel best?
How can I rise to meet you?
What is the name of Reginn?
What is the relationship to reign?
Who is the rider and who is the ridden?

Anglo-Saxon Rune Poem

> Rad byþ on recyde rinca gehwylcum
> sefte ond swiþhwæt, ðamðe sitteþ on ufan
> meare mægenheardum ofer milpaþas.

Dickins Translation

> Rad
> Riding seems easy to every warrior while he is indoors
> and very courageous to him who traverses the high-roads
> on the back of a stout horse.

My Translation

> Journey dwells at house warrior every
> Soft and very active, that sits on above
> Horse very strong over milestone road.

Icelandic Rune Poem

> Reið er sitjandi sæla
> ok snúðig ferð

ok jórs erfiði.
iter ræsir.

Dickins Translation

Reid - Riding
Joy of the horsemen
and speedy journey
and toil of the steed.

My Translation

Riding is seated bliss
And swift journey
And steed effort.
Glorious starter.

I could not find *iter* in the Concise Dictionary, but instead turned to *ítr*, which means "glorious, excellent."

Norwegian Rune Poem

Ræið kveða rossom væsta;
Reginn sló sværðet bæzta.
Reidh

Dickins Translation

Riding is said to be the worst thing for horses;
Reginn forged the finest sword.

My Translation

Riding speaks of horses worn out by wet and toil;
The gods struck swords best.

The word *baezta* does not appear in the dictionary. Instead I found the word *bezt*, or "best."

Week 6: KENNAZ

Inquiry for KENNAZ

Sacred light and burning—where is the intersection of these?
Pain and illumination—where is the intersection of these?
Flesh and mortification—where is the intersection of these?
How do you receive visitors in a diseased house?
What is the opening?
Where do you close?
What offerings may pacify an angry god?
What offerings do you receive?
What is the price of freedom?
What is the stone of sovereignty?
Is there a torch needed in the cave?
Is the luminous always corrupt?
Where is the intersection of these?

Anglo-Saxon Rune Poem

> *Cen byþ cwicera gehwam, cuþ on fyre*
> *blac ond beorhtlic, byrneþ oftust*
> *ðær hi æþelingas inne restaþ.*

Dickins Translation

> *Cen*
> *The torch is known to every living man by its pale, bright flame;*
> *it always burns where princes sit within.*

My Translation

> *Torch is alive each, known with fire*
> *Bright and light, burns often*
> *There princes within cease from toil.*

Icelandic Rune Poem

> *Kaun er barna böl*
> *ok bardaga [för]*

ok holdfúa hús.
flagella konungr.

Dickins Translation

Kaun – Ulcer
Disease fatal to children
and painful spot
and abode of mortification.

My Translation

Boil is children distress
And battle journey
And flesh decay house.
Flight king.

Flagella is a Latin gloss for "whip," but there is an Icelandic word, *flaug*, which means "flying" or "flight."

I could not find *holdfúa* as one word, but *hold* is "flesh" and *fúa* is "decay."

Norwegian Rune Poem

Kaun er barna bǫlvan;
bǫl gǫrver nán fǫlvan.

Dickins Translation

Kaun
Ulcer is fatal to children;
death makes a corpse pale.

My Translation

Boil is children's curse;
Misfortune makes corpse wither.

Week 7: GEBO

Inquiry for GEBO

Where are you present?
Where are you absent?
What is the sacrifice?
What is the gift?
Where is the state of being balanced?
How are the offerings to be made?
How does the receiving happen?
Is this a dance or a drudgery and what makes the difference?
Where is difference welcome?
Where is the sacred available in exchange?
What do you ask of me?
What do you ask of my people?
What should I ask of myself?
What should I ask of my people?
How do we make reparations?
Where are you present?
What is the gift?

Old Anglo-Saxon

There is only one rune poem for GEBO in Old Anglo-Saxon:

> Gyfu gumena byþ gleng and herenys,
> wraþu and wyrþscype and wræcna gehwam
> ar and ætwist, ðe byþ oþra leas.

Dickins Translation

> Gyfu
> Generosity brings credit and honour, which support one's dignity;
> it furnishes help and subsistence
> to all broken men who are devoid of aught else.

My Translation

Gift man is honor and praise,
Support and worship and uplift each
Glory and substance, thee shall be other untrue.

I could not locate wyrdscype but did find *weorþscipe*, meaning "worship."

Week 8: WUNJO

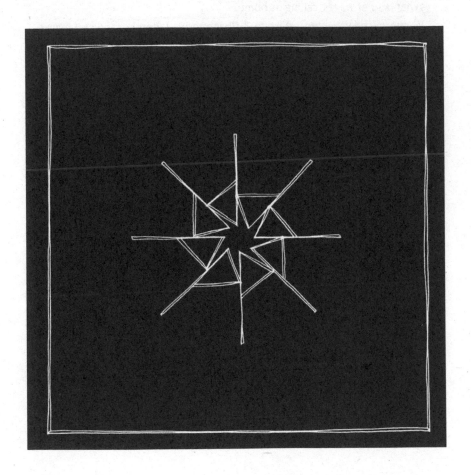

Inquiry for WUNJO

Wunjo my heart, where is the joy?

How does it travel, the mountains of my ancestors so far away?

Wunjo, my heart, what seeds need planting?

What banner waves, calling us home?

Wunjo, my heart, where is the altar? What offering falters so far do we roam?

Wunjo, this feeling—the open and blooming, the call unassuming—can you translate this day?

Where would you have me?

What would you have me do?

How is celebration both an honoring and a death?

Is joy possible after so much pain?

Wunjo, my heart, we ask in refrain, repeating our questions again and again.

Anglo-Saxon Rune Poem for WUNJO

> Wenne bruceþ, ðe can weana lyt
> sares and sorge and him sylfa hæfþ
> blæd and blysse and eac byrga geniht.

Dickins Translation

> Wynn
> Bliss he enjoys who knows not suffering, sorrow nor anxiety,
> and has prosperity and happiness and a good enough house.

My Translation

> Hopeful enjoyment, thee a knowledge believe little
> Suffering and distress and them self have
> Blade and rejoicing and with dwelling abundance.

Week 9: HAGALAZ

Inquiry for HAGALAZ

What is the nature of the hailstorm?
Where do you find it coldest?
The measure of pain is what?
How is the melting significant?
What offerings do you take?
What offerings do you reject?
Where is the reaping place?
How do we understand the turning point?
Where do you begin?
Where do you end?
What is the nature of destruction?
How do we begin?

Anglo-Saxon Rune Poem

Hægl byþ hwitust corna; hwyrft hit of heofones lyfte,
wealcaþ hit windes scura; weorþeþ hit to wætere syððan.

Dickins Translation

Hail is the whitest of grain;
it is whirled from the vault of heaven
and is tossed about by gusts of wind
and then it melts into water.

My Translation

Hail is whitest grain;
Turns it from heavens aerial,
Rolls it winds a shower; worthless it to water since.

Icelandic Rune Poem

Hagall er kaldakorn
ok krapadrífa
ok snáka sótt.
grando hildingr.

Dickins Translation

Hagall - Hail
Cold grain
and shower of sleet
and sickness of serpents.

My Translation

Hail is cold grain
And shower of sleet
And snake sickness.
Do harm hero.

Norwegian Rune Poem

Hagall er kaldastr korna;
Kristr skóp hæimenn forna.

Dickins Translation

Hail is the coldest of grain;
Christ created the world of old.

My Translation

Hail is cold becoming grain;
Christ mocking heaven ancient.

I could not find *skóp*, but instead *skop* in the CDOI, which means "mocking," and *skap* which means "condition/shape/form." Also for *haeimenn*, I found *himinn/himnar* in CDOI which means "heaven."

Week 10: NAUDHIZ

Inquiry for NAUDHIZ

What is the needfire?
Where is creation most fed by constraint?
How do I make my lessons?
Where is peace?
Who receives the offering?
What is the ritual?
What is ancestral medicine from the bow drill?
What is the relationship of the Nornir?
Where is fire in my life?
Where is necessity in my life?
What is the intersection of these with the needfire?
What is the boon of NAUDHIZ?

Anglo-Saxon Rune Poem

Nyd byþ nearu on breostan;
peorþeþ hi þeah oft niþa bearnum
to helpe and to hæle gehpæþre,
gif hi his hlystaþ æror.

Dickins Translation

Trouble is oppressive to the heart;
yet often it proves a source of help and salvation
to the children of men, to everyone who heeds it betimes.

My Translation

Necessity is narrow with breast;
Fate game them, yet often to envy burned
To help and to a brave man terrible station,
A gift them his listen before.

Peorþeþ or *peorð* is another rune whose meaning is uncertain. I feel it is "pouch" or "game pieces," or perhaps the runes themselves. I translate it here as "fate game."

I could not find *gehþæþre*, and so I went with *gehþ*, which means "a station," and *ǽ-þreclic* which means "terrible."

Icelandic Rune Poem

> Nauð er Þýjar þrá
> ok þungr kostr
> ok vássamlig verk.

Dickins Translation

> Constraint
> grief of the bond-maid
> and state of oppression
> and toilsome work.

My Translation

> Necessity is
> Bondswoman yearning
> And heavy choice
> And toil loathsome work.

Since I could not find vássamlig, instead I chose *vás* and *ámátligr*, meaning "toil" and "loathsome."

Norwegian Rune Poem

> Nauðr gerer næppa koste;
> nøktan kælr í froste.

Dickins Translation

> Constraint gives scant choice;
> a naked man is chilled by the frost.

My Translation

> Necessity building near cost;
> Naked what is in frost.

Week 11: ISA

Inquiry for ISA

Who is the container?
Who is the contained?
What is the most ancient form?
Where were you in the beginning?
Where do you end?
How do you hold the runes?
What do you find within the ice?
Where are the shapes within us?
How do we discover the offering?
What is the lesson of the frozen?
What is the lesson of the lost?
How does this apply to us now?
What is the container?

Anglo-Saxon Rune Poem

Is byþ ofereald, ungemetum slidor,
glisnaþ glæshluttur gimmum gelicust,
flor forste geworuht, fæger ansyne.

Dickins Translation

Ice is very cold and immeasurably slippery;
it glistens as clear as glass and most like to gems;
it is a floor wrought by the frost, fair to look upon.

My Translation

Ice is exceedingly old, immensely slippery,
Glisten clear as glass to put forth gems similar,
Floor frost wrought, beauty face.

Icelandic Rune Poem

Íss er árbörkr
ok unnar þak

ok feigra manna fár.
glacies jöfurr.

Dickins Translation

Ice
Bark of rivers
and roof of the wave
and destruction of the doomed.

My Translation

Ice is bank of a river
And wave bed cover
And fated to die man harm.
Glacier king.

Norwegian Rune Poem

Ís kǫllum brú brœiða;
blindan þarf at lœiða.

Dickins Translation

Ice we call the broad bridge;
the blind man must be led.

My Translation

Ice call bridge melt;
Blind necessity at lead.

Reflections on the First Third
Rune Connection and Ancestral Healing

As we conclude this eleventh week of meditation practice, it is helpful to reflect on the first third of the journey, to see where there might be opportunities for a deepening relationship with the runes or healing and also to notice where there are barriers to contact.

In my journeys with the runes I have found many barriers to knowing them that originated in ancestral wounding. Deep in my lineage is a powerful thread of fear around magic, divination, and the occult. In working with others on this path, I have found that fear to be persistent—so much so that it obscures gnosis. If you are experiencing fear or having difficulty connecting with the rune beings in this practice, the following exercises can help you acknowledge and integrate your own ancestral wounds.

Part of our work in holding simultaneity is to see things not as healed or unhealed, but rather as a journey of integration and transference. Healing is endless and active. As we work in healing, we can find our gifts in the wounds and the wholeness of possibility in holding space for both.

In order to clearly view the wounds in our lineage, we must first understand their origin. As humans we stand very close to history and the attendant trauma, grief, estrangement, and complications present in lineage work. These manifest in a number of emotional reactions. I list them here in a litany, that we may absolve them and witness their power.

Exercise 1: Litany of Ancestral Emotions

The word *litany* is an ancient one for "prayer." This exercise is intended to be used in ritual to express a variety of ancestral emotions. You may explore the emotions in whatever mode speaks to you most: reading aloud, singing, dancing, art, or writing. As you work you might notice emotions intensely, but try to resist holding on to them. The goal of this exercise is to create a clear channel for emotional transportation, to see them traveling *through* us. It doesn't mean they are gone or disposed of, just released, like the bowl that overflows with too much water then dumps into a clear flowing stream.

Not all of these emotions may apply to you personally, and in this we widen the scope of our ancestral work from the self. Please speak or sing the emotions anyway, because it is likely in your billions of ancestors you have someone who has experienced them. Please speak or sing them for your sisters, brothers, and nonbinary kin of this earth. We speak and sing for self and each other.

Also, please include any other emotions you feel need a voice to clear, and feel free to change the words in a way that authentically reflects your own truth.

Emotion: Fear

We sing the emotion of fear to release this barrier to connection. With self, with health, with ancestors, with spirit, with earth, with death, with birth. Oh wind, water, earth, and sun, help us sing fear until it is done.

Emotion: Shame

We sing the emotion of shame to release this barrier to connection. With self, with health, with ancestors, with spirit, with earth, with death, with birth. Oh wind, water, earth, and sun, help us sing shame until it is done.

Emotion: Rage

We sing the emotion of rage to release this barrier to connection. With self, with health, with ancestors, with spirit, with earth, with death, with birth. Oh wind, water, earth, and sun, help us sing rage until it is done.

Emotion: Pain

We sing the emotion of pain to release this barrier to connection. With self, with health, with ancestors, with spirit, with earth, with death, with birth. Oh wind, water, earth, and sun, help us sing pain until it is done.

Emotion: Avoidance

We sing the emotion of avoidance to release this barrier to connection. With self, with health, with ancestors, with spirit, with earth, with death, with birth. Oh wind, water, earth, and sun, help us sing avoidance until it is done.

Emotion: Estrangement

We sing the emotion of estrangement to release this barrier to connection. With self, with health, with ancestors, with spirit, with earth, with death, with birth. Oh wind, water, earth, and sun, help us sing estrangement until it is done.

Emotion: Loss

We sing the emotion of loss to release this barrier to connection. With self, with health, with ancestors, with spirit, with earth, with death, with birth. Oh wind, water, earth, and sun, help us sing loss until it is done.

Emotion: Powerlessness

We sing the emotion of powerlessness to release this barrier to connection. With self, with health, with ancestors, with spirit, with earth, with death, with birth. Oh wind, water, earth, and sun, help us sing powerlessness until it is done.

Emotion: Envy

We sing the emotion of envy to release this barrier to connection. With self, with health, with ancestors, with spirit, with earth, with death, with birth. Oh wind, water, earth, and sun, help us sing envy until it is done.

Emotion: Grief

We sing the emotion of grief to release this barrier to connection. With self, with health, with ancestors, with spirit, with earth, with death, with birth. Oh wind, water, earth, and sun, help us sing grief until it is done.

Exercise 2: Ancestral Narratives and the Witch Wound

In working toward wyrd path connection, I realized that at the epicenter of emotions around ancestral reconnection is what I call the *witch wound*. The more I study the transitions in Europe from tribal communities to state systems, from pre-monetary systems to capitalism, from matristic power-shared systems to patriarchal power over, from pre-racist identification to the creation of white supremacy, the more I understand my own colonial culture. These ideologies that began at a time of change and crisis then spread out like pestilence to other cultures around the world. These ideologies were most fervently exposed for the delusion they are during the witch hunts. The hunted and the hunter both bear the witch wound.

The witch wound roots in every person. In people of European descent the witch wound divides, is rooted in necessary division. The witch wound separates women from their power, separates men from the feminine, denies the nonbinary, and carries a legacy of unbelievable violence, hatred, greed. The witch wound speaks only in duality: right/wrong, good/evil, self/other, rich/poor, divine/not, so it was easy to apply to cultures beyond. Colonialism is the witch wound. Sexism is the witch wound. Racism is the witch wound. The witch wound is globalization. The witch wound is earth degradation. The witch wound is speciesism. The witch wound is religious superiority. The witch wound is fear. It opened culturally in a psychological sequence, the same temporal arena as land privatization, the rise of Christianity as a state religion, the advent of large-scale slavery, the colonization of so-called new worlds. These are all connected.

Where does the witch wound live in you? In me it comes up as chronic anxiety, my fear of potency and visibility, and waves of disconnected, unearned shame. How do we heal? We must travel back in ancestral memory, before the advent of this culture—far before. We must remember through the clues in story and myth, archaeological evidence seen through eyes absent the lie of "progress," through landscape, through reclaiming a living, animist, collectively diverse worldview. We heal when we live into nonlinearity, community, sovereignty, activism, action, solidarity, regeneration, reparations, and deep listening to the wounds of others. Liberation from dominant culture and its insistence on historical superiority is dependent on addressing the witch wound. We must remember, reweave, live into the source.

The runes can help us connect to our ancestors prior to the witch wound. If you have ancestors from colonized countries, there may be more resources in the collective memory and work being done to reconstruct these precolonial ways and heal lineage through cultural regeneration.

For those of us with European ancestry, whether it is our identity or not, we have to go back much further in our ancestral myths and symbols to connect with the folkways and earth-revering cultures of our ancestors. Much of the evidence has been deliberately destroyed.

To address the witch wound is to decondition ourselves from modern industrial culture and to deny the myth of "it was always this way." And this requires ancestral connection, because our preindustrial, precapitalist, pre-Christian, pre-patriarchal, precolonial ancestors can remind us of the old lifeways, which belong to all of us, which live in our blood and bones. Our deep ancestors can help us reach those parts of ourselves that remember. They can help us find the patterns in history that knotted so thoroughly to allow our disconnection, our separation.

How do we do this work?

We already are.

In rune practice we make space to research and understand the knots in our ancestral wyrd, the witch wound, and to move back beyond it to a time before such a knot was present. This exercise continues this work through narrative inquiry, research, and writing. For example, if the women in your family were abusive to each other, then you might look for examples of matristic, cooperative societies in the far reaches of your lineage. It is not easy work, but finding some academic evidence for symbols, stories, archaeology, or anthropology that reflect some aspect of your healing is deeply empowering. As you find resources, you can begin to construct a story—a myth, fairy tale, or nonfiction narrative—showing what healing can look like, visioning your lineage forward by showing what was once present in the past.

As with the runes, you may need to travel into the Neolithic or Paleolithic to find answers, ancestors untroubled by the witch wound. I have included some resources from my studies at the end of this book, but the world is vast and my knowledge not comprehensive. So you must travel, uncover, and research where you are drawn. There is also an element of play in this, imagination, to take one thread and vision it a pattern. Don't be afraid to make things up in your story where research is thin. You might be surprised by what you find when you allow yourself imaginative freedom.

If you come from multiple ethnicities and are unsure of where to start, go first where you are drawn, then see if there are any parallels between your lineages. Resistance—the place you are not excited about—is sometimes an indication of necessary pursuit, too, however uncomfortable. But begin where your heart takes you. I have found it useful to explore each lineage separately but with regularity—I devote time every year to the distinctive branches of my ancestors, their languages and cultures, then try to find both the nuances and syncretic beliefs between them as I investigate an area of ancestral interest like folk medicine or the runes.

If you are adopted or estranged from your family of origin and unsure of your biological ancestry, you may choose to pursue where you are drawn, your assumed ancestry, your adopted ancestry... we have so many ancestors, many of whom were fostered outside of/without knowledge of their biological culture. Calling on the ancestors to begin guiding your dreams, the serendipity of your research, and the stories you create can bring forward some that support/empathize with your desire to connect from a unique position. You are not alienated, your ancestors—known or not—hold you.

Your research and imagination lay the foundation for a new narrative in your family lineage, the witch wound healed, your descendants living in ways that align with earth reverence, peace, bounty, and boundlessness. You may wish to tell this story as an oral tale, or write it as a letter to your descendants, a letter to your ancestors, a myth or a fairy tale. It may be repeated many times and from different points of view. Keep a record of your process, both research and creative, as you explore over time and watch what begins to transform in your life and awareness.

As always, ritualizing these exercises helps create an energetic container for their potency and communicates on levels outside of conventional consciousness—exactly where the ancestors work.

The runes as beings can be a supportive force in ancestral healing. As vibrational pieces of the web of wyrd, with connection to the weavers of fate—layers of ørlög and wyrd crafted by the Norns—they can assist in this process of healing and reclaiming.

Week 12: JERA

Inquiry for JERA

Where is the turning?
Where do we experience the wheel?
Is the wheel multiple?
What else spins?
How can we feel these cycles in our lives and work?
What is the harvest?
Where is the growth?
How does plenty inform both?
What is my life without trust in the turning?
Is there a time that is separate from our conceptions?
What will you teach us about the movement of the days?
JERA, sacred is the motion as we dwell in your ways.

Anglo-Saxon Rune Poem—In Old Anglo-Saxon

Ger byþ gumena hiht, ðonne God læteþ,
halig heofones cyning, hrusan syllan
beorhte bleda beornum ond ðearfum.

Dickins Translation

Ger
Summer is a joy to men, when God, the holy King of Heaven,
suffers the earth to bring forth shining fruits
for rich and poor alike.

My Translation

Year is a man hope, when God one let go,
Consecrated the sky ruler, the earth gives voluntarily
Of bright blood burning and need.

Icelandic Rune Poem—in Old Icelandic

Ár er gumna góði
ok gott sumar

algróinn akr.
annus allvaldr.

Dickins Translation

Ár – Plenty
Boon to men
and good summer
and thriving crops.

My Translation

First beginning is sons of men good
And good summer
The lush field.
Year sovereign.

Norwegian Rune Poem

Ár er gumna góðe;
get ek at ǫrr var Fróðe.

Dickins Translation

Ar
Plenty is a boon to men;
I say that Frodi was generous.

My Translation

First beginning is sons of men good;
Get I at swift spring knowledge.

I could not find *var*, only *vár*, and I chose to translate the name Fróðe which means "knowledge."

Week 13: EIHWAZ

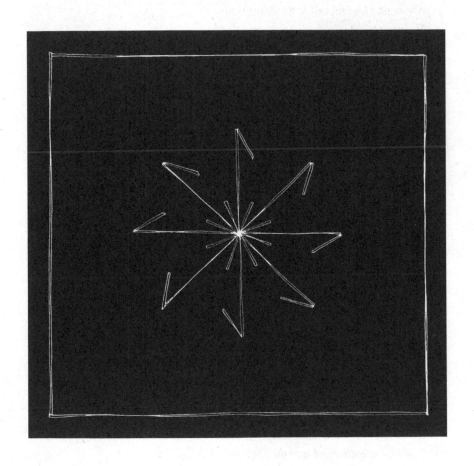

Inquiry for EIHWAZ

Sacred yew, which is my direction?
How does above relate to below?
How does below relate to above?
Where do I find myself in this transition?
Are you a tree?
Are you a hook?
What is the nature of the rooted?
What is the nature of the branch?
What is the nature of the death that is life?
Where should I take a chance?
Holy relic, how do I sacrifice?
Ancient container, where is my offering?

Norwegian and Icelandic Rune Poems

There are no Norwegian or Icelandic rune poems for EIHWAZ.

Anglo-Saxon Rune Poem

> Eoh byþ utan unsmeþe treow,
> heard hrusan fæst, hyrde fyres,
> wyrtrumun underwreþyd, wyn on eþle.

Dickins Translation

> The yew is a tree with rough bark,
> hard and fast in the earth, supported by its roots,
> a guardian of flame and a joy upon an estate.

My Translation

> Yew is from without not smooth a tree,
> Hard the earth fixed, guardian firs,
> Herb freedom sustaining, joy on a home.

I broke down the word *wyrtrumun* into two words: *wyrt* and *rumun*. I could not find *rumun*, so I went with *rúmian*, meaning "freedom."

Week 14: PERTHO

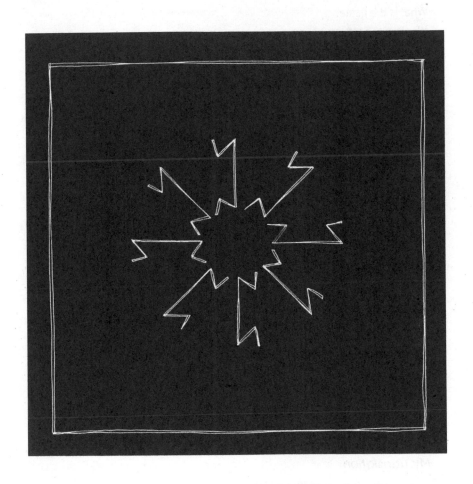

Inquiry for PERTHO

Who is the keeper of the space within?
What does it mean to lose?
What does it mean to win?
What is the game?
Who are the players?
How does this become gestation?
How does this become birth?
What offerings do you receive?
What wisdom do you offer?
Is this chance or fate?
Who is the keeper?
What is kept?
Are you the well?
Are you the water?
What do you contain?
What do you excuse?

Anglo-Saxon Rune Poem

There is only an Anglo-Saxon rune poem for PERTHO.

> Peorð byþ symble plega and hlehter
> wlancum [on middum], ðar wigan sittaþ
> on beorsele bliþe ætsomne.

Dickins Translation

> Peordh
> Peorth is a source of recreation and amusement to the great,
> where warriors sit blithely together in the banqueting-hall.

My Translation

> Fate game is always play and laughter
> Proud with middle, where do battle to sit
> With feasting hall joyful together.

Week 15: ALGIZ

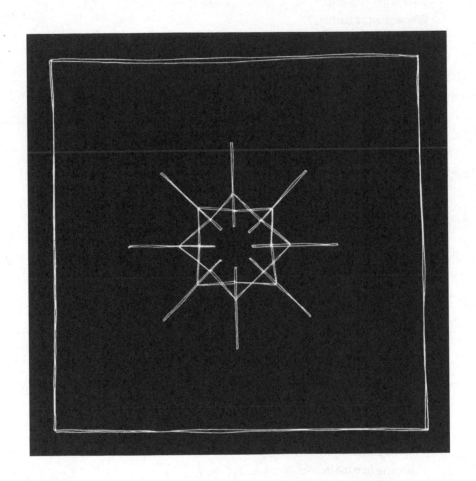

Inquiry for ALGIZ

What is protection?
What is a protector?
What is protective, at what cost and what price?
Who is the challenge?
Where are the barriers?
Who holds the blood?
What is the offering?
How is it held?
Where in the marshes do we find the flood?
How is there standing amid it all?
Who has the resources for sharing?
Is there protection in the call?

Anglo-Saxon Rune Poem

Eolh-secg eard hæfþ oftust on fenne
wexeð on wature, wundaþ grimme,
blode breneð beorna gehwylcne
ðe him ænigne onfeng gedeþ.

Dickins Translation

Eolh
The Eolh-sedge is mostly to be found in a marsh;
it grows in the water and makes a ghastly wound,
covering with blood every warrior who touches it.

My Translation

Elk sword land source often in fen
wax in water, wound grim,
blood burns on fire each
particle him substantial laying hold of dead.

Week 16: SOWILO

Inquiry for SOWILO

Ancient one, how ancient are you?
What do you remember from the beginning of time?
How is the miracle of life even possible?
In the flare, in the solar, in the sky, beyond, who is your kindred?
As sister, as daughter, as friend, who is your kin?
As shape, as texture, as color, who do you ken to?
As wonder, as worship, as offer, who lets you in?
What songs should we sing in the season of planting?
What songs should we sing as the ice melts again?
What songs should we sing at the season of ending?
How do we keen the death of the sun?
What can we know of the world, rebegun?

Anglo-Saxon Rune Poem

Sigel semannum symble biþ on hihte,
ðonne hi hine feriaþ ofer fisces beþ,
oþ hi brimhengest bringeþ to lande.

Dickins Translation

Sigel
The sun is ever a joy in the hopes of seafarers
when they journey away over the fishes' bath,
until the courser of the deep bears them to land.

My Translation

The sun to load ever shall be with hope,
Then it members of a household carry over fishes to wash,
Until it a sea horse brings to land.

Icelandic Rune Poem

Sól er skýja skjöldr
ok skínandi röðull

ok ísa aldrtregi.
rota siklingr.

Dickins Translation

Sól - Sun
Shield of the clouds
and shining ray
and destroyer of ice.

My Translation

Sun is clouds shield
And shining glory
And ice age difficulty.
Heavy rain king.

I could not find *aldrtregi*, and instead used *aldar*, "age," and *tregi*, "difficulty."

Norwegian Rune Poem

Sól er landa ljóme;
lúti ek helgum dóme.

Dickins Translation

Sun is the light of the world;
I bow to the divine decree.

My Translation

Sun is land shining;
Bow down I holy judgment.

Week 17: TYR

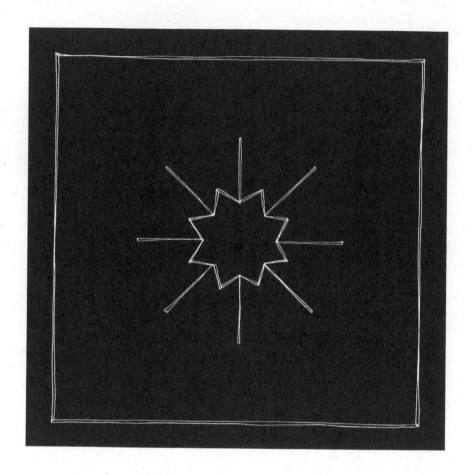

Inquiry for TYR

Where are you pointing?
That is the way?
What is the promise made in the shape?
Tell me about before the spear, what begins?
Tell me about after the spear, what ends?
Where is the essence of relationship?
How are such bonds forged?
What is the nature of betrayal?
Is truth the same as justice?
Is a lie the same as love?
Who is responsible for oaths broken?
What is the power of an oath unspoken?
What is the power of a promise made in word?
Who is the creature calling?
What can be heard?

Anglo-Saxon Rune Poem

Tir biþ tacna sum, healdeð trywa wel
wiþ æþelingas; a biþ on færylde
ofer nihta genipu, næfre swiceþ.

Dickins Translation

Tir

Tir is a guiding star; well does it keep faith with princes;
it is ever on its course over the mists of night and never fails.

My Translation

Glory is a sign some, to watch over a covenant well
Towards princes; always is with journey
above night mist, never wanders.

Icelandic Rune Poem

Týr er einhendr áss
ok ulfs leifar
ok hofa hilmir.
Mars tiggi.

Dickins Translation

Tyr
God with one hand
and leavings of the wolf
and prince of temples.

My Translation

Tyr is one-handed old heathen god
And wolf's leavings
And heathen temple chief.
Mars noble.

Norwegian Rune Poem

Týr er æinendr ása;
opt værðr smiðr blása.

Dickins Translation

Tyr
Tyr is a one-handed god;
often has the smith to blow.

My Translation

Tyr is a one-handed god;
often has the smith to blow.

I could not find *æinendr* but instead found *ein* meaning "one" and *endr* meaning "end" in the CDOI. But then I uncovered a reference that it means "one-branched." I could not find other evidence to support this.

Week 18: BERKANA

Inquiry for BERKANA

Who nurtures the soil?
Who tends the land?
Who sees the green?
What is the keeper of all unseen?
Who is the giver?
Who also receives?
How does it matter, the twigs and the leaves?
Where is the guardian of the sacred gate?
What roots can we find, if we are not too late?
Dance with the soil, dream with the dance;
Berkana, what rhythm calls the song of chance?

Anglo-Saxon Rune Poem

> Beorc byþ bleda leas, bereþ efne swa ðeah
> tanas butan tudder, biþ on telgum wlitig,
> heah on helme hrysted fægere,
> geloden leafum, lyfte getenge.

Dickins Translation

> Beorc
> The poplar bears no fruit; yet without seed it brings forth suckers,
> for it is generated from its leaves.
> Splendid are its branches and gloriously adorned
> its lofty crown which reaches to the skies.

My Translation

> Birch tree is void of bleeding; bears even as yet
> Branches out of fertile, is with dye radiant,
> Lofty with crown cover decorated beauty,
> To grow leaves, the sky close to.

Icelandic Rune Poem

Bjarkan er laufgat lim
ok lítit tré
ok ungsamligr viðr.
abies buðlungr.

Dickins Translation

Bjarken – Birch
Leafy twig
and little tree
and fresh young shrub.

My Translation

To help is leafy open foliage
And not much trees
And young vast forest.
Rising one prince.

The word *Bjarkan* is not in the CDOI. *Birki* is the word for "birch tree" in Old Icelandic.

These words are related to *Bjarkan*:

Bjarg means "rock" or "boulder."

Bjarga means "to help or save."

Bjargrúnar are runes for helping women in labor.

I am choosing to translate *Bjarkan* as *Bjarga*, "to help."

Laufgat breaks down into *lauf,* "leafy," and *gat,* "open."

Abies is not in the CDOI but is Latin and means "rising one." It is used to describe a fir tree.

Norwegian Rune Poem

Bjarkan er laufgrønstr líma;
Loki bar flærða tíma.

Dickins Translation

Birch has the greenest leaves of any shrub;
Loki was fortunate in his deceit.

My Translation

To help is leaves verdant mortar;
Flame needles deceit time.

Loki is often translated as *logi,* "fire or burning." Interestingly though, *lok* means "bolt," and *lokka/lokkan* means "to allure/entice." *Varðlokkur* are magic songs to entice the spirits (from *varð,* "guarantee," and *lokkur,* "entice"). *Lok* also means "fern or weed," which may relate to Loki's mother Laufey, whose name implies leaves.

I could not find the word *bar,* but *barr* means "needles" like those of coniferous trees.

Week 19: EHWAZ

Inquiry for EHWAZ

What is the rush of the sacred companion?
Where in the species do you dwell?
How can we find our roving rhythm?
When we find it, how will we tell?
What is the dance of hillside or valley?
What offerings are made at the start of a course?
In depth ritual there once was a knowing.
A people of people, a horse of a horse.
Who in my ancestors can I call to remember?
What was a name for this time before time?
Beyond the mechanics of daily labor,
In transport, in intimacy, in rhythm, in rhyme?

Anglo-Saxon Rune Poem

There is only one historical rune poem for EHWAZ.

> *Eh byþ for eorlum æþelinga wyn,*
> *hors hofum wlanc, ðær him hæleþ ymb[e]*
> *welege on wicgum wrixlaþ spræce*
> *and biþ unstyllum æfre frofur.*

Dickins Translation

> *Eh*
> *The horse is a joy to princes in the presence of warriors.*
> *A steed in the pride of its hoofs,*
> *when rich men on horseback bandy words about it;*
> *and it is ever a source of comfort to the restless.*

My Translation

> *War horse is earl isle of nobles delight.*
> *A horse court proud, there him hero about*
> *Rich in people on horse to change speech*
> *And is not still ever comfort.*

Week 20: MANNAZ

Inquiry for MANNAZ

In the matrix of the sacred, where is the joinery?
Whose union is the base of creation?
What synergy is your offering?
What synthesis is your music?
Where does the bridging take place?
In the compromise, what is erased?
The function of human/man/woman is kind, but which is the symbol of divine mind?
What color do you bring?
What shape is your sound?
What is the generosity of the host?
How do we celebrate?
What matters most?

Anglo-Saxon Rune Poem

Man byþ on myrgþe his magan leof:
sceal þeah anra gehwylc oðrum swican,
forðum drihten wyle dome sine
þæt earme flæsc eorþan betæcan.

Dickins Translation

Mann
The joyous man is dear to his kinsmen;
yet every man is doomed to fail his fellow,
since the Lord by his decree will commit the vile carrion to the earth.

My Translation

People is with mirth his kinswoman beloved:
A band yet one each other deceiver,
Even a ruler will judgment a sight
The poor flesh earth to show.

Icelandic Rune Poem

> Maðr er manns gaman
> ok moldar auki
> ok skipa skreytir.
> homo mildingr.

Dickins Translation

> Madr – Man
> Delight of man
> and augmentation of the earth
> and adorner of ships.

My Translation

> Human being is man's pleasure
> And mold's increase
> And to arrange ornament.
> Man a liberal man.

Skip means "ship," but *skipa* means "to arrange" or "to unload."
Homo is Latin.

Norwegian Rune Poem

> Maðr er moldar auki;
> mikil er græip á hauki.

Dickins Translation

> Madhr
> Man is an augmentation of the dust;
> great is the claw of the hawk.

My Translation

> Human being is mold's increase.
> Great is malice of a hawk.

I could not find *græip* in the CDOI. Instead I found *græð*, which means "malice."

Week 21: LAGUZ

Inquiry for LAGUZ

Sacred flow, where do you wander?
Sacred know, what is the source?
Sacred well, where is the beginning?
Sacred leek, what is the wrapping?
Laguz, do you speak to depth?
What are the waters you represent?
Where is the wisdom of the beginning?
What is the mystery of the seed?
How do I keep my rites in the cycle?
Laguz, how do I ask when I'm in need?
Where should I listen?
What should I heed?

Anglo-Saxon Rune Poem

> *Lagu byþ leodum langsum geþuht,*
> *gif hi sculun neþan on nacan tealtum*
> *and hi sæyþa swyþe bregaþ*
> *and se brimhengest bridles ne gym[eð].*

Dickins Translation

> *Lagu*
> *The ocean seems interminable to men,*
> *if they venture on the rolling bark*
> *and the waves of the sea terrify them*
> *and the courser of the deep heed not its bridle.*

My Translation

> *Sea is people long abundant,*
> *A gift it owes to venture on boat unstable*
> *And it sea wave strong give fear*
> *And the sea horse of a bridle not heed.*

Icelandic Rune Poem

Lögr er vellanda vatn
ok viðr ketill
ok glömmungr grund.
lacus lofðungr.

Dickins Translation

Lögr – Water
Eddying stream
and broad geysir
and land of the fish.

My Translation

Sea is boiling water
And forest cauldron
And shining ale green field.
Award prince.

I could not find *glömmungr* in the CDOI. Instead I found *glom*, meaning "shine," and *mungr* meaning "ale." *Lacus* is Latin and means "award."

Norwegian Rune Poem

Lǫgr er, fællr ór fjalle
foss; en gull ero nosser.

Dickins Translation

Logr
A waterfall is a River which falls from a mountain-side;
but ornaments are of gold.

My Translation

Water is frightening from mountain
Waterfall; and gold be costly thing.

Fæla is "to frighten"; *faella* in modern Icelandic is "phobia."
Falla is "to fall."

Nosser is not in the CDOI and does not appear in modern Icelandic as spelled. *Hnossir* means "costly thing or ornament" in Old Icelandic; in modern Icelandic *Hnoss* means "lucky" and *Hnossir* means "desirable."

WEEK 22: INGWAZ

Inquiry for INGWAZ

Sacred seed, holy soil, where is the evidence of our toil?
What can we learn of lineage?
In shape, where do we see sacrifice?
What is your relationship to divinity?
Where can I feel you most?
Where can I feel you least?
What is the burden of the seed?
What is the story of the seeded?
Is there a song I can sing at sprouting?
Is there a lament for reaping?
How do we weave this cycle?
Where do we find your will?
Sacred seed, holy soil, where is the evidence of our toil?

Norse and Icelandic Rune Poems

There are no Icelandic or Norse rune poems for INGWAZ

Anglo-Saxon Rune Poem INGWAZ

Ing wæs ærest mid East-Denum
gesewen secgun, oþ he siððan est
ofer wæg gewat; wæn æfter ran;
ðus Heardingas ðone hæle nemdun.

Dickins Translation

Ing
Ing was first seen by men among the East-Danes,
till, followed by his chariot,
he departed eastwards over the waves.
So the Heardingas named the hero.

My Translation

A meadow existed first with east valley
To see to say, until he afterwards grace

Over sea departed; a swift chariot after robbing;
Thus brave, bold men the health named.

Ing is most often translated as a name, but sticking to the work of Kvilhaug I chose to translate it by its meaning, which is "meadow." Similarly, *east denum* is always translated as East Danes, but the word for Dane, *Dene*, means "valley." *Secgun* is not in the OASD. *Secgan* is and means "to say."

   Heardingas is also translated as a name and is not in the OASD, but *hearding* is in the OASD and means "brave, bold men."

   Nemdun does not appear in the OASD. *Nemde* means "to name" in plural.

Second Third Reflection
Rune Connection and Animist Earth Wisdom

Wights and Place-Based Ancestor Work

As we wend through the second third of our wyrd path, you may have noticed the specific attunement of many runes with the elements of nature and earth cycles. As we take space for reflection, we journey into the realms of the animate world, into relationship with the most ancient aspect of ancestral connection, a memory inherent in the runes, the land itself. Land-based ancestor work can be a balm . . . but here in North America where I live, the concept of land as ancestor is wrapped into intersectional oppressions and directly derivative from the witch wound. It was wounding that sent most settlers across the sea, that colonized and actively perpetrated genocide in the Americas. This wound extends to contemporary culture in the deep division and impoverishment in settlers, of life disconnected from life.

The earth is our common ancestor. In the deepest matrix of human knowing, the mythic, the unconscious, the symbolic, we remember this. Science is continually unfolding the potential for all life's emergence from a single cell, our oldest common ancestor in this story a bacterium named LUCA (an acronym for last universal common ancestor). But beyond science there is this reality: the bones of our ancestors rest in the earth, as will we, as will our descendants. We eat of them daily. The bones of all life rest in the earth. We eat of all life daily. We are a part of an infinitude of processes, micro and macro, that bring us into relationship with all that is. In this re-membering, the web of life expands, and our own existence becomes part of a vastness. We are no longer striving alone for connection; we have always been connected.

The option for integrating land-based ancestor work into your runic experience is experiential, to journey with our ancestors both human and nonhuman, to travel in inquiry and openness to a state of animist conversation.

What Is Animism?

Animism is, simply, a belief in life—that all of this world and nature is animated by life force. Some animists call this spirit, others call it Gaia consciousness. Whatever the language there is an essence of enchantment in animism, the ability to interact with the spirits, deities, or sentience of the earth itself. I have explained to my children that I am an animist because it makes life more rich and full, more possible and interesting. For logical folks, animism may require stepping out of contemporary dualistic thinking and into a new reality that can hold things as being real and not real simultaneously.

For children, animist belief is a natural state. Modern culture with its capitalist modeling requires a suspension of animist beliefs; we couldn't exploit creatures and places—or even other people—so thoroughly if we believed them to be part of a living spiritual matrix, the same as us. It is much easier to destroy what is seen as inferior, unconscious, and inanimate and, therefore, understandable that we would be schooled to de-animate the world. Animist belief in modern times has been collectively relegated to the arena of dismissive nutty and/or insidiously discriminatory (for example, the belief that animist cultures are somehow inferior to modern, industrial cultures and get in the way of progress). Returning to a place of wonder in relationship with the natural world brings us closer to our ancestors. They may speak to us through plants, stones, landscapes, animals, and rivers, and we can orient ourselves to their skills and crafts through better understanding the places where we live.

Here I offer meditations/inquiry sessions to build or deepen our conscious relationships with the elements, plants, animals, and nonhuman spirits—called *wights* in my tradition, or *vættir*—and end with a ritual from the Northern European tradition called *útiseta*, or "sitting out."

If you live in an urban environment, all of these practices can be engaged with on a micro level. There is no need for "purity" of nature to commune with the ancestral spirits connecting all.

There are a number of resources offered at the end of this book for exploring concepts such as bioregionalism and visuals for viewing the matrix of ancestors from a Jungian perspective.

Exercise 1: Meditation for Connection

This meditation may be used throughout the week to connect and clear you.

Breathe deeply, reach out consciously.

Imagine you have roots. Begin to push them into the soil. Allow them to move around boulders and obstructions, drift them down until you locate a source of underground water, a clear running stream.

Dip your roots into the stream and flow. This is the essence of place, ever present and nourishing. This is Nerthus, the sacred earth blood, veiled and waiting. Draw your blood up through the roots, let it enter your veins and body as the shimmering web of wyrd. Let it heal and anneal all the old wounds.

See the veins of your body as the shimmering web of wyrd. Allow the stream to find the knots in your body and pour sweet, clear, healing energy into the knots. Bring the stream into your brain, dive deep into the microcosm of your electric nerve center. There the stream blooms electric too, healing and annealing all the harm within your brain.

Allow the waters to emerge gently now through your pores and skin, see them carrying away an ancient pain of disconnection, soothing and washing you clean and clear in the bounty of timeless repair.

This is your ancestors, bathing you and loving you.

This is your Dísir, bathing you and loving you.

This is the earth, bathing you and loving you.

Notice what comes as you allow yourself to be one with the earth.

Notice symbols and sounds.

See yourself outside yourself, as the earth sees you, as the bones of your ancestors see you, as your Dísir see you: as most precious vessel of the lineage, healer of the witch wound, keeper of the sacred creative that flows easily and wholly through you.

You are clear and healthy, whole and loved. The flow never stops, the clearing never ceases. Everywhere you are the earth, everywhere you are this energy. Open your eyes and make an offering, a single prayer for all that sustains you. Then close your ritual in blessing and write what you have received.

Exercise 2: Útiseta, Sitting Out

Many runes the cold has told me,
Many lays the rain has brought me,
Other songs the winds have sung me;
Many birds from many forests,
Oft have sung me lays in concord
Waves of sea, and ocean billows,
Music from the many waters,
Music from the whole creation,
Oft have been my guide and master.

—From the Finnish epic poem, the *Kalevala*,
translated by John Martin Crawford[40]

At its simplest level, útiseta is a ritual practice for natural immersion and receiving information.

It has a long history of magical associations and was used for communion with the dead as well. It was outlawed in Iceland due to Christian perspectives on magical/pagan/earth-based spiritual practice.

For the purposes of our explorations, útiseta is a way to remove ourselves from the human sphere, to go into a natural space alone even if it is only a yard, and sit out for a period of time—traditionally it was overnight but I fully recognize the pragmatics in this—with an open heart, a central question, and a soul intent on communication.

I introduce this practice as it, like many spiritual practices from my ancestors, is relatively unknown. It is mentioned as a tool used for contemplation, decision-making, and receiving spiritual information from the dead. Thorgeirr in Iceland "sat out" beneath a skin for a day and a night to determine whether Iceland should Christianize. In the Edda poem *Svipdagsmol*, Svipdag "sits out" on the grave mound of his mother to gain instruction. In the Concise Dictionary of Old Icelandic it is defined as "sitting out in the open air" and has a relationship to magical practice. These sources have informed my interpretive practice of útiseta, which involves sitting overnight in a natural environment and/or "going under the cloak," that is, covering my head to reduce sensory input as I meditate or journey.

A few suggestions:

You may choose to sit out during a particular time of ancestral significance, such as a solar holy day or a phase of the lunar cycle, or it could simply be when you desire connection with the land spirits or ancestors.

As you prepare to sit out, consider bringing an offering for the land and its beings. This could be something simple: food prepared with your own hands, drink collected with your ancestors in mind. I often share oat cakes, apples, and herbal tea in ritual with the land spirits and share my meals daily with the wights in my home.

You may choose to further exercise your senses by "going under the cloak" as you sit out, as these are complementary practices in the recorded lore. I live in an urban area, so this has an added benefit of blocking ambient light when I sit out at home.

Your primary intention should be clear. Is it to introduce yourself to the beings of the land where you live? To ask your ancestors about land-based practice? Form a cohesive question in your mind as you enter the space.

Use your intuition to know when the ritual is through. Close with blessings. Ask your ancestors to guide your work and words as you deepen your relationship with the beings of your place.

I don't give specific, step-by-step ritual instructions for this exercise for a reason: each of us can find our own way to sit out, and so much of this wyrd path is trusting our intuition, developing spiritual sovereignty. As with the rune practice, the primary ingredients in any ritual are time, intention, offering, and listening to develop relationship. Every time I practice útiseta, I am drawn into a new ceremonial structure, informed by my continual exploration of ancestral traditions and the communication I receive in dreams. If this is not your path, see what other natural immersive practices exist in your ancestral traditions. Removal from the human world and connection with the spirits of nature form a common cord through many cultures. The beings and spirits of your land and lineage will support you in finding a way to this practice, and deepening a relationship with the land spirits will expand your relationship with the runes. There is no one way, only a way of reverence and devotion.

Week 23: DAGAZ

Inquiry for DAGAZ

Who hails the day?
What is at the center?
Where is transformation?
How does it move?
Where am I in motion?
What is the most ancient form?
Are you the last, or next to last, a culmination or a near culmination?
How has this changed me?
What is the motion of power?
Where is the shape at the center?
Are you the embodiment or the embodied, the tool or the keeper of tools?
How do you dawn?
What is required to rule?

Anglo-Saxon Rune Poem

Dæg byþ drihtnes sond, deore mannum,
mære metodes leoht, myrgþ and tohiht
eadgum and earmum, eallum brice.

Dickins Translation

Dæg
Day, the glorious light of the Creator, is sent by the Lord;
it is beloved of men, a source of hope and happiness to rich and poor,
and of service to all.

My Translation

A day is lord messenger, beloved man,
Boundary maker light, mirth and hope
Prosperous and poor, all useful.

Week 24: OTHALA

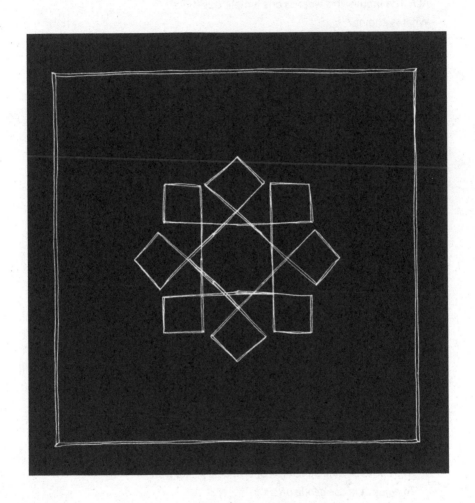

Inquiry for OTHALA

This week we complete a sacred cycle with the closure of the Elder Futhark. There is some disagreement with how this cycle ends—with DAGAZ or OTH-ALA. The inquiry this week is one simple question:

What is ending?

To further the exploration:

How many answers can OTHALA bring to this question?

How many ways can you explore ending in your life?

What are the relationships between DAGAZ and OTHALA?

If you started at the beginning and are working your way through this class, what are your reflections on the past twenty-four weeks?

What has changed? What is the same?

This is a good time to revisit your intentions for this practice, and perhaps create some new ones as we travel into our last nine weeks with the Anglo-Northumbrian runes.

Anglo-Saxon Rune Poem

Eþel byþ oferleof æghwylcum men,
gif he mot ðær rihtes and gerysena on
brucan on bolde bleadum oftast.

Dickins Translation

Ethel
An estate is very dear to every man,
if he can enjoy there in his house
whatever is right and proper in constant prosperity.

My Translation

Inheritance is exceedingly dear every man,
A gift he to be able there right and what is fitting with
To enjoy at house gentle often.

The Anglo-Northumbrian Runes

The next nine runes are wild with mystery. Sometimes referred to as the Anglo-Saxon or Anglo-Northumbrian runes, they rarely appear in books about the runes, and it can be difficult to find a rune set with them included. Five are named in the Anglo-Saxon rune poem, but four are found only in manuscripts or on artifacts and are thus referred to sometimes as "pseudo-runes." Some scholars see this as evidence of their insignificance; others see the opposite—a unique potency in these particular runes.

These are the runes where my gnosis became vital and where I learned an important lesson about UPG explorations: it is best vetted by both research and community. I initially explored the runes in a group class facilitated by someone who borrowed heavily from a gnosis-based author. So I was indoctrinated into the perspective that these runes were more ancient than the Elder Futhark and given meanings for the runes rooted in this perspective. After I left the group and began my own research, however, I learned that the likelihood of ancientness pertains to all of the runes, and their emergence at different times in different social contexts is the result of a number of factors. By translating the rune names and rune poems I came into a deeper understanding of these runes for myself, and while their power does not exclude earlier perspectives (who am I to deny another's gnosis?), by sourcing these runes in archaeology, myth, and language I've found a stronger sense of both the runes and myself.

I also learned the value of community exploration rooted in research. In sharing both gnosis and research, the live Gnosis Group component of this journey at the Wild Soul School helped affirm some of my experiences with the Anglo-Northumbrian runes in such a way that when I craft rune sets now I know to never leave them out.

There is some overlap in the rune names, meanings, and even poetic resonance. As you travel, try to allow for simultaneity and mythic both/and. Ancestral ways are not exclusive; there is room for all in our journey.

Week 25: AC

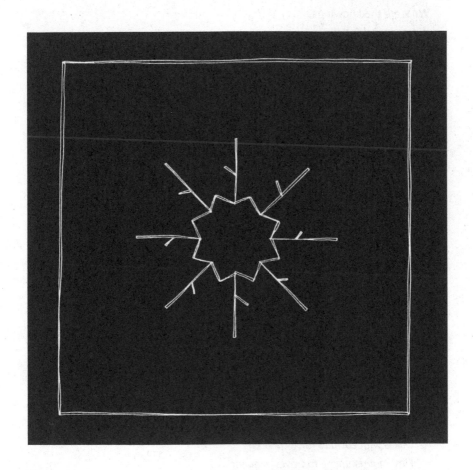

Inquiry for AC

Is the shape a telling?
What is the oak?
What is the forest?
What are the knowings?
Where is the cycle?
What is the calling?
What is ocean?
What is faith?
Where is the offering?
What is the knowing?
Where are you going?
In earth, in wraith?

Anglo-Saxon Rune Poem for AC

Ac byþ on eorþan elda bearnum
flæsces fodor, fereþ gelome
ofer ganotes bæþ; garsecg fandaþ
hwæþer ac hæbbe æþele treowe.

Dickins Translation

Ac
The oak fattens the flesh of pigs for the children of men.
Often it traverses the gannet's bath,
and the ocean proves whether the oak keeps faith
in honorable fashion.

My Translation

Oak is with earth to tarry children
Flesh nourishment, to travel frequent
Over water fowl's bath; the ocean tests
Whether oak possesses homeland trust.

Week 26: OS

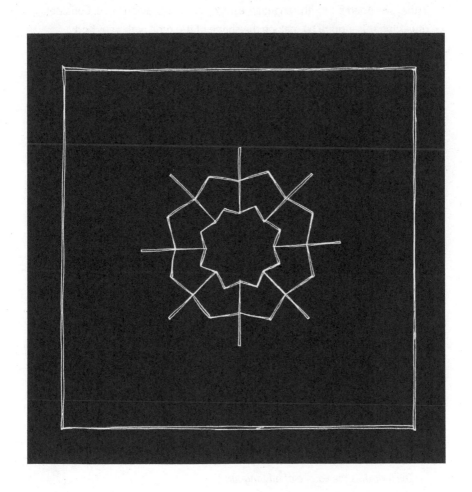

Inquiry for OS

This week's inquiry begins a little differently—I don't know the whys of these, only that they ask for presentation.

The primary question of relationship with OS has to do with its symbols in the rune poems: mouth, language, estuary, scabbard, sword, god. Consider ritualizing this inquiry by making the shape of the rune with your body:

Both arms bent and upright, an offering, a beseeching, a receptacle. Feel the energy of OS in your body, draw into it with permission. Feel into the symbols that resonate with you. Then ask of OS: *What is your role in my life?*

The answer may come immediately or may be present through the week . . . It may be relational, interactive, intellectual . . . or it may not come at all. Is this an answer too?

There is no wrong way to receive.

OS Rune Poems

Explorations with OS, as with so many of the ancient rune forms, draw us into simultaneity. The name of ANSUZ in the rune poems is OS, yet they are presented as separate runes with similar connections. So here we study the ANSUZ/OS poems again, seeking relationship and nonlinear coalescence. I translated these poems at a different time than the ANSUZ poems and have found it useful to notice what changed and what remained the same in my interpretations, how this may be applied to my understanding of this rune as distinct.

Anglo-Saxon Rune Poem

Os byþ ordfruma ælere spræce,
wisdomes wraþu ond witena frofur
and eorla gehwam eadnys ond tohiht.

Dickins Translation

Os
The mouth is the source of all language,
a pillar of wisdom and a comfort to wise men,
a blessing and a joy to every knight.

My Translation

> God is beginning healing plant speech
> wisdom help knowledge comfort
> and earl every one happiness and trust

I struggled with the word *ælere*, which appears to translate directly only as several potential plant names including marjoram, fleabane, and elecampane, so I gave it context as healing plant, rather than name a plant specifically.

Icelandic Rune Poem

> Óss er algingautr
> ok ásgarðs jöfurr,
> ok valhallar vísi.
> Jupiter oddviti.

Dickins Translation

> Óss - God
> Aged Gautr
> and prince of Ásgardr
> and lord of Vallhalla.

My Translation

> River's mouth is perfect bragging
> and Ásgard's king
> and Vallhalla leader
> Jupiter leader

Norwegian Rune Poem

> Óss er flæstra færða
> før; en skalpr er sværða.

Dickins Translation

> As
> Estuary is the way of most journeys;
> but a scabbard is of swords.

My Translation

River mouth most brings
Journey; and scalp is sword.

Week 27: YR

Inquiry for YR

Who is the arrow?
What is the bow?
Where in my body do I know what you know?
How to pull taut?
How to take aim?
How to focus with breath and let loose?
What is the yew?
What is the season?
When we reach the target, how will we see?
Whose relationship do you honor?
What offerings do you receive?
Why do we fail?
Why do we trust?
Where is the center of the cycle?

Anglo-Saxon Rune Poem

Yr byþ æþelinga and eorla gehwæs
 wyn and wyrþmynd, byþ on wicge fæger,
 fæstlic on færelde, fyrdgeatewa sum.

Dickins Translation

Yr
Yr is a source of joy and honour to every prince and knight;
it looks well on a horse and is a reliable equipment for a journey.

My Translation

A bow is heroes and earls every one
Delight and honor, is on a steed beautiful,
Firm with a journey, warlike armor some.

Icelandic Rune Poem

Ýr er bendr bogi
 ok brotgjarnt járn

ok fífu fárbauti.
arcus ynglingr.

Dickins Translation

Yr - Yew
Bent bow
and brittle iron
and giant of the arrow.

My Translation

Yew tree is bent bow
And breaking eager iron
And fool harm beater
Arrow young person.

I could not find *brotgjarnt* in the CDOI. Instead I combined *brot,* "breaking," and *gjarn,* "eager." I could not find *fífu,* but *fífl* means "fool or clown," and *fífu* in contemporary Icelandic means "cotton grass tussocks." I could not find *fárbauti* in the dictionary. *Fár* means "harm" and *bauta* means "beater." Fárbauti is also the giant father of the trickster god Loki. *Arcus* is Latin for "arrow."

Norwegian Rune Poem

Ýr er vetrgrønstr viða;
vænt er, er brennr, at sviða.

Dickins Translation

Yr
Yew is the greenest of trees in winter;
it is wont to crackle when it burns.

My Translation

Yew tree is winter pine tree to furnish wood;
To give one hope of where, is to burn with a flame, that burning.

Sviða in contemporary Icelandic means "divisions."

Week 28: IOR

Inquiry for IOR

Who is the secret?
Who is the sea?
Who is the fish aligning both?
Where do we travel in the between?
What is the vision?
What does all mean?
Transformation and challenge, enjoyment and sustenance, where is the relationship between the all?
What is the offering?
How is it made?
When is the beginning of the motion?
Where is the cross that transcends?
Who is the secret?
Who is the sea that mends?

Anglo-Saxon Rune Poem

Iar byþ eafix and ðeah a bruceþ
fodres on foldan, hafaþ fægerne eard
wætre beworpen, ðær he wynnum leofaþ.

Dickins Translation

Ior
Iar is a river fish and yet it always feeds on land;
it has a fair abode encompassed by water, where it lives in happiness.

My Translation

Eel is a river fish and yet always enjoys
Fodder on the earth, it has beautiful native soil
Water cast down, where he joyfully sustains.

Week 29: EAR

Inquiry for EAR

What is the transition between life and death?
After decomposition, what part is left?
Where is the connection between self and grave?
Who needs saving and what can be saved?
How in my life can I be aware of rot?
What offerings open the door to the root and decay?
What is the necessity of coming close to death?
Where is the connection between grave and earth?
Where is the connection between grave and birth?
Why is the wisdom toward letting go?
Why is the letting go a point of growth?
What do I need to let go of now?
What is the transition between life and death?

Anglo-Saxon Rune Poem

> Ear byþ egle eorla gehwylcun,
> ðonn[e] fæstlice flæsc onginneþ,
> hraw colian, hrusan ceosan
> blac to gebeddan; bleda gedreosaþ,
> wynna gewitaþ, wera geswicaþ.

Dickins Translation

> Ear
> The grave is horrible to every knight,
> when the corpse quickly begins to cool
> and is laid in the bosom of the dark earth.
> Prosperity declines, happiness passes away
> and covenants are broken.

My Translation

> The ground is hideous earl each,
> When firm flesh sets about,
> A body becomes cold, the earth chooses

Bright to consort; to bleed to fall,
Delight to behold, to stir together to cease from proceeding.

In the Bosworth-Toller OAS Dictionary *Ear* means "sea," "ocean," "an ear of corn," and "ear" and "a harrow." *Éar* means the rune and "wave," though the Old English translator says it means "the earth" and "the ground."

Week 30: CWEORTH

Inquiry for CWEORTH

Where can I find the source?
What is the rhythm?
Where is the turning?
What is your true name?
Is it in grinding?
Is it in burning?
Where is the matrix of loss to earth?
Where is the center?
What is the birth?
Where should I leave an offering?
What do we forget as the mill ceases turning?
Who is the memory of something before?
Cweorth, what is patience to revealing more?

Linguistic Associations

There are no rune poems for CWEORTH, yet the form is ancient, echoing in the patterns of Old Europe long before the runes became an alphabet. Here are some linguistic associations with the most closely related Anglo-Saxon words from the Bosworth-Toller Anglo-Saxon Dictionary:

cweorn

   e; f: cweorne, an; f. *A mill, hand-mill, quern*

cweorn-bill

   es; n. [bil a bill, falchion] *A stone chisel for dressing querns; lapidaria*

cweorn-burna

   an; m. *A mill-stream*

cweorn-stána

   mill-stone

cweorn-téþ

   pl. m. *Molar teeth, grinders; molares,*

Week 31: CALC

Inquiry for CALC

What is the offering?
Where is the earth?
How can we distinguish the death from the birth?
How can we hallow that which is unknown?
Where is the compound of shell and of bone?
Who is the secret that lives on the land?
Where is the memory?
Where do we stand?
How do we make ceremony amid so much loss?
What is returning?
What does depart?
How to protect what lives in our heart?
Who are the ancestors that remember this call?
Where do we meet them in your sacred hall?

Linguistic Associations

There are no traditional rune poems for CALC.

In the Bosworth-Toller Anglo-Saxon Dictionary, CALC is defined as "a shoe, or little sandal" and "chalk."

Chalk formations and deposits are part of the ancient geological history of Northern and Western Europe. In Britain there are a number of large chalk figures, including the Uffington White Horse, which is dated to the Late Bronze Age.

Week 32: STAN

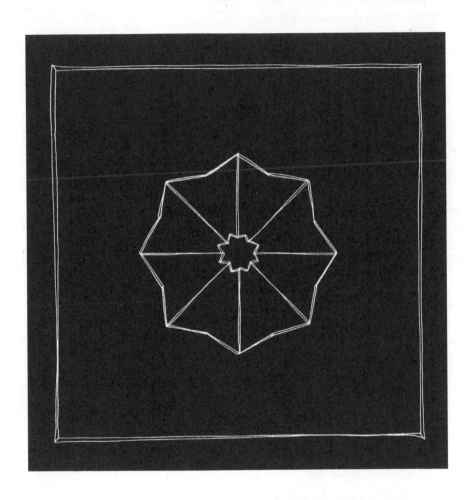

Inquiry for STAN

What is the relationship between stand and stone?
Where do we travel together alone?
What is the better way to enter the earth?
How can we measure a life of worth?
What is the secret of the circles tall?
What is the language, the stone's call?
Where do we dig and where do we break?
What do we venture and what do we make?
Who knows the history whispered by stones?
How can we find the chamber of bones?
What do we recognize in your form?
Where do we leave your offerings?
Where is the place of the stone songs?
Why do we remember so little?
How can we begin from this stand?

Linguistic Associations

There are no traditional rune poems for STAN.

In Old Anglo-Saxon the word *stán* means "stone" as a material.

The Bosworth-Toller Anglo-Saxon Dictionary includes a host of words that begin with *stan*, for example:

Stánœx: stone axe

stán-bæþ: stone bath--steam bath with water poured on hot stones

stán-beorh: stone hill

stán-berende: stone bearing

stán-bill: an implement of stone

stán-boga: stone arch

Other related words include:
stanc: a sprinkle

stand: a stand, stay, pause, delay

Week 33: GAR

Inquiry for GAR

What is the piercing?
Where is the tip?
How is the sharpness related to rip?
Where is the veil?
What is the spear?
How can we learn to trust what we hear?
Who is the thrower?
Who is the prey?
What comes from the future but answers away?
Where is the mystery?
How is the gift?
What is the portent we read from this rift?
Who is the keeper of secrets divine?
How can we know what is yours and is mine?
Where is the place where offerings lay?
What is the memory we invoke in this day?

Linguistic Associations

There are no traditional rune poems for GÁR.

In the Bosworth-Toller Anglo-Saxon Dictionary, *gár* is defined as: "A dart, javelin, spear, shaft, arrow, weapon, arms or weapon with a pointed head."

Related words include:

gára: a spear man or pointed strip of land

gare: ready, finished

Reflection on the Third
Runic Connection and Ancestral Reverence

Remembering the Old Ways

In our weeks together we have traveled through the cellular mysteries of our own motherline, reached into the web of wyrd to identify knots and tears in our lineage threads, and rooted into land and place to broaden our perspective of time and self. To reflect on this last third of what is, I hope you sense, a perpetual journey, we will be gathering patterns for reverence, tending the bones, and nourishing this work in the sacred everyday of our lives. In this way we continue to nurture relationship with the beings of the runes, the web of wyrd that is all creation, and the ancestral wisdom we carry in our bodies.

In order to do this, we must come home to our humanness and reach into the well of our common past.

Ancestor reverence is a human universal. As Lyle Steadman puts it in "The Universality of Ancestor Worship," "the focus on differences has caused an apparently universal aspect of religion to be overlooked: the claim that ancestors influence the living and are influenced by the living. We argue here that claims of communication between the dead and their descendants are universal and may be key to understanding the universality of religious belief."[41]

So the ancestors are important. And communicating with them—and them with us—is one of the key components of human experience. Expanding our view of ancestors to include places and other species allows us another variety of human experience: that of connectedness with all life. We feel it in our very cells, this call to wholeness. How can we integrate ancestral communication and veneration into our lives? How can we begin to remember and revere what is so fundamental to our humanity?

It is through continuing the practice of inquiry—in which, if you have completed even a portion of the thirty-three-week wyrd path journey, you are well versed—that we become oriented to the spectrum of our ancestry. It is the myth of modernity and secularism that has divided us from our lineages, along with a pantheon of fears, wounds, and pain. To heal we must reweave our ancestral memory. This is lifework and involves attempting to view the world from the perspective of our ancestors, to vision old-new ways of being.

Reclaiming Ancestral Ways and Skills

The first exercise/meditation/work of our integration is to practice questioning the aspects of ancestry that exist in our everyday lives to find new ways and rhythms to focus our practice. By integrating the dreams, beliefs, skills, and rituals of our ancestors into daily practice, we continue to open and awaken to their wisdom.

These questions may be asked of a particular topic on a daily basis, or you may wish to take this exercise slowly, devoting a week or more to the inquiries of each section.

You are also welcome to devise your own inquiry ritual for any area missing from this catalog. As with all in this book, it is not meant to be comprehensive but rather a beginning. If we can see the patterns of our ancestral wyrd through the transitions that mark human experience, we may begin reclaiming and transforming lives of meaning and alignment.

When we begin to reclaim and devote ourselves to learning ancestral ways, our ties to both past and future strengthen—the threads rewoven, the pattern true.

Ancestral Ways of Living: Remembering as Medicine

For the healing, this may be a written exercise, an art project, a meditation, a dance, a prayer. Ask your ancestors how they would like you to express information, then craft a ritual for your unique, cocreative expression as you engage with the following questions. You will see that these explorations are quite expansive. How you interact with them will be on a spectrum between intuitively and concretely. I encourage you to research the topics that speak to you to help you understand more deeply your ancestors' experiences and how those experiences can apply to our world today.

Ancestral Ways of Dying

How did your ancestors die? What did they think happened to the body and spirit after death?

What are some death rituals and practices in your ancestral tradition(s)?

How did they treat the body?

What was the role of the living in death?

What is the history of death practices in your ancestral tradition(s)? Where were colonial, patriarchal, religious, and/or institutional norms instituted? When and at what time?

How does your family experience death? Are they accepting and open? Avoidant and pained?

What are the intersections between the experiences of your family and the experiences of your ancestors?

What speaks to you in the process of reclaiming ancestral death practices?

What repels or stokes your fear in the process of reclaiming ancestral death practices?

How did your ancestors treat their elders?

What position did elders hold in the community?

What is the history of elders in your ancestral tradition(s)? Where were colonial, patriarchal, religious, and/or institutional norms instituted? When and at what time?

How are the elders treated in your family?

What is your relationship with elders and aging?

What are the intersections between your ancestral practices around elders and your family?

How can your ancestors be honored in familial nourishment, practices, rituals, and traditions around aging and death?

Ancestral Ways of Birthing

How did your ancestors give birth?

What is the history of birthing practices in your ancestral tradition(s)? Where were colonial, patriarchal, religious, and/or institutional norms instituted? When and at what time?

How did your mother give birth?

What are the intersections between the two experiences?

What speaks to you in the process of reclaiming ancestral birthing practices?

What repels or stokes your fear in the process of reclaiming ancestral birthing practices?

How can your ancestors be honored in familial nourishment, practices, rituals, and traditions around pregnancy, childbirth, and postpartum caring?

Ancestral Ways of Education

How were your ancestors educated?

What is the history of educational practices in your ancestral tradition(s)?

Where were colonial, patriarchal, religious, racist and/or institutional norms instituted? When and at what time?

How were your parents educated?

What are the intersections between the two experiences?

How were you educated?

How are your children educated?

What do you wish for in the education of yourself and your children?

Where can you see new hope for educational transformations in culture today?

What speaks to you in the process of reclaiming ancestral educational practices?

What repels or stokes your fear in the process of reclaiming ancestral educational practices?

How can your ancestors be honored in service, support, or expansion of educational ideas right now?

How did ancestral education practices relate to work?

What was the definition of work for your ancestors? When did colonial, patriarchal, religious, and/or racist institutional norms begin to inform your ancestor's work?

What are your attitudes about work?

Where do you see hope for a way of work in alignment with ancestral traditions?

What prevents you from claiming an ancestral relationship to work?

How can you begin to bring your work into alignment with your ancestral connections?

Ancestral Ways of Ritual and Celebration

How did your ancestors celebrate the cycles of the seasons, the holy days, the rhythm of the year?

What is the history of ritual practices in your ancestral tradition(s)? Where were colonial, patriarchal, religious, and/or institutional norms instituted? When and at what time?

What is your parents' relationship to ritual and celebration? Are they spiritual or secular? Is there a division between the two?

What are the intersections between the experiences of your parents and your ancestors?

How do you experience ritual and celebration?

How do your children experience ritual and celebration?

What do you wish for in ritual and celebration for yourself and your children?

Where can you see new hope for celebration transformations in culture today?

What speaks to you in the process of reclaiming ancestral ritual practices?

What repels or stokes your fear in the process of reclaiming ancestral ritual practices?

How can your ancestors be honored in service, support, or expansion of ritual ideas right now?

Ancestral Crafts and Skills

What did your ancestors make? What are some skills and crafts from your lineage tradition(s)?

What is the history of craft practices in your ancestral tradition(s)? Where were colonial, patriarchal, religious, and/or institutional norms instituted? When and at what time?

What are your parents' relationships with craft and skills? Are there any particular talents in your parents' lineage? Are there any stories of deficiency?

What are the intersections between the experiences of your parents and your ancestors?

How do you experience craft and the development of skills?

How do your children experience craft and the development of skills?

What do you wish for in learning or deepening crafts and skills for yourself and your children?

Where can you see new hope for crafts and skills in culture today?

What speaks to you in the process of reclaiming ancestral craft practices?

What repels or stokes your fear in the process of reclaiming ancestral craft practices?

How can your ancestors be honored in service, support, or expansion of craft and skill ideas right now?

Ancestral Medicine

How did your ancestors experience medicine and healing? What are some areas of wisdom in your lineage tradition(s)?

What is the history of medicine in your ancestral tradition(s)? Where were colonial, patriarchal, religious, and/or institutional norms instituted? When and at what time?

What are your parents' relationships with medicine? Are there any particular areas of health in your parents' lineage? Are there any stories of illness?

What are the intersections between the experiences of your parents and your ancestors?

How do you experience medicine, health, and healing?

How do your children experience medicine, health, and healing?

What do you wish for in learning or deepening experiences in medicine and healing for yourself and your children?

Where can you see new hope for medicine in culture today?

What speaks to you in the process of reclaiming ancestral health practices?

What repels or stokes your fear in the process of reclaiming ancestral health practices?

How can your ancestors be honored in service, support, or expansion of medicine and health practices right now?

What is missing from these inquiry categories? Create your own category along with your own questions for exploration.

In Blessing: Remembering our Sacred Name

In our ending, our beginning. Bringing the process full circle, we return home to ourselves. After your explorations through the runes over the course of our practice, what do you experience when you come back to this essential question:

What is your true name?

As we see with the names of the runes, words hold power and also provide a key to vast supplies of information. In translating the proper names in the rune poems we receive a new depth of information and power not available elsewhere.

One of the traditions we are least likely to question is that of patrilineal naming. It is one of the most extraordinary assumptions in recent human history that we have always named our children after the father's line. In fact, surnames are a relatively contemporary invention, with many variations the world over. My own family surnames were often place-based, which was common in Europe after the advent of the feudal system, or patronymic/matronymic names, as are still common in Iceland. Our ancient ancestors had more relational, community, and land-based ways of identifying themselves, and it makes sense as we begin to unravel the oppressive threads of capitalism, colonialism, and patriarchy that we would question a tradition rooted in all of these.

In addition to place-names and community names, our ancestors had sacred names, craft names, names that identified them with their offerings in the world. There are a number of coming of age and rites of passage rituals that convey this kind of empowered naming, where the name conferred is chosen by the person, rather than parents or partners or some outside authority.

This is all to say that naming is potent, an early magic. Finding the language for who we are and what we do is part of claiming our lineage as a whole.

What languages did your ancestors speak?

What is your name story?

How does it relate to your ancestors?

Do you identify with your name?

What is your name for what you do, for your craft or work?

I am a person of many names: legal names, personal names, hidden names, working names, and magical names. My first name was given to me by my mother at birth and honors many ancestors. My hidden middle name is both my mother's name and my great-grandmother's name and so honors my motherline. After my divorce, when I first began working with women's mysteries, I took the name Vesta as my surname, honoring my maiden name, which was Vestnys, meaning "West Bay" in Norwegian (a name conferred on my paternal ancestor on immigration as his family name was patrynomic) and invoking the ancient fire goddess Vesta.

As I continued my spiritual journey deeper into ancestry, I was guided over many years to take the name Veleda, to claim a potent part of history and raise awareness about the oracular magic of my Germanic ancestors. Veleda was a priestess of the Bructeri tribe. Of her the Roman Tacitus wrote, "The Germans traditionally regard many of the female sex as prophetic, and indeed, by an excess of superstition, as divine. This was a case in point. Veleda's prestige stood high, for she had foretold the German successes and the extermination of the legions."[42] Her name may have been a title—and its meaning is debated—but the roots in elder languages speak to seeing and power. As a Germanic title, with a potentially Proto-Celtic root, the name Veleda synthesizes my motherline which is German, Irish, and Scottish.

At first I was uncomfortable with taking my own names. My family, the men in particular, were taken aback and hurt. But eventually it became an easeful, commonplace piece of who I am. Challenging assumptions is never easy, but believing in the support and celebrations of my ancestors has helped considerably.

Too often we don't feel a kinship with our personal name. So we borrow names from other cultures or feel stuck with names from a dominant culture.

In order to travel with our ancestors, we must each make our way to their wisdom, their earth ways, their language, their names.

How does this feel to you? Where do you notice resistance?

• • •

As we arc around to conclude this circle of wyrd ancestor work, explore the power of your name. Discover/inquire as much as you can about your ancestral names and delve into the potential of who you are.

What do you call yourself, ancestor to the future?
What is your sense of your own name? Where does it come from?
Do you subscribe to the tradition of patrilineal naming? Why or why not?
What names have you always been drawn to?
What names hold particular power for you?

With every word, with each naming, you make a magic for generations to come.

How to End and Begin Again
My Runic Journey

I began my journey with the runes alone—taking classes, sure, yet being dependent on the knowledge of others, a "good student" of the runes, an academic deferring to "experts." This gave me some useful fundamentals, but it also led me far away from my own relationship to the runes. It wasn't until I connected with others on the path through the Wild Soul Runes Gnosis Group, a collective of individuals sharing gnosis in relationship while working through this 33-week meditation, that my work opened up and the gnosis deepened considerably. When I began this book, I had no intention of offering my views on each of the runes, but after talking with some of the gnosis group members, I realized having other perspectives can help affirm our own.

I include these at the end of the book, rather than interwoven in the primary text, so those who wish for only a personal gnosis experience can proceed uninterrupted. But once you conclude your own journey, if you wish, you may begin again. I've chosen to present this next portion as a backward transport. Opposing forces were considered to be very powerful in ancient times, and traveling a path backward had a new, specific kind of potency.

These are my thoughts only, a direct record of my experience through the Wild Soul Runes practice. They are in no way definitive. I do not answer the questions I asked of the runes, rather, I record impressions, make associations, and lead into a sensibility of feeling. They are an offering to the divine, the spirits, the earth itself.

GAR

The piercing that is a gift, contained within the sacred seed, GAR is INGWAZ cracked open by rain or fire or the summer wind. It feels like sex, like the tip of the spear cresting the aperture of universal fabric that is the feminine. In the absence of the piercing, though, a motion, the veils thin or torn, allowing us to see from one world into the next.

GAR carries the endless masculine energy of Oðin riding forth into mystery, the willing sacrifice, the warrior. It reminds me of an ancient magic, captured in the Merseburg healing charm, where like cures like: bone to bone, blood to blood. This complementary sense of healing and harming, piercing and mending is GAR's communication this season.

In terms of comprehension, though, GAR is ever-changing, elusive, resisting any attempt to capture or harness. It is a portal built on will and without bound, vast as the universal fabric in which it appears.

STAN

Monolith on the moor, ancient sentinel, the barrier that is also a portal—STAN is an impediment in my reading, a barrier, a boundary, a way marker that will frustrate before it reveals. But with careful tending, STAN becomes a door: a fissure appears down its middle and within its center lies the other worlds.

STAN has also appeared as a headstone, a memorial, apparition of the grave. Something buried here needs tending. More than any other rune, STAN is metamorphic, the fruit of ice and fire at the beginning of time, contained within the memory of life before life. It represents the patience that is geological time, for in passage all things change, even stone, if only very slowly.

CALC

Pour out your offering to the infinite sea. This is your beginning, and it is also me. CALC is the cup that is also a spear, the stone that is soft, the study in contrasts that bridges the binary in its insistence on sacrifice.

This is a rune whose meaning feels sacred to the sea. When I first encountered CALC, I saw a trident. I was told by my teacher it wasn't so, but the image persisted and the feeling was true. The first meaning of its name I knew was chalk, that strata of sea life millions of years old. Chalk is soft in its age, white in color, can be carved and dusted into shape but will not hold it long. Malleable, permeable CALC sends a message about offering: it can be anything and is impermanent; it must be continually renewed.

But CALC is also a small sandal, a little shoe, a protective diminutive, essential to walking. Perhaps this too is offering, may be shielding and even slight. However done, CALC asks us to heed the call.

CWEORTH

CWERN: Mill; to grind; to transform, make nourishing, reduce. This is a death rune, make no mistake. The goddess Hel grinds souls in her cauldron, transforming them, so they may flow into the rivers of the world and be reborn into a new form. But I was always taught this was a rune of fire, rune of the funeral pyre, but this makes no sense given its etymology.

However, ancestors know the mill. Milling grain for porridge and flour was essential to transforming culture. Prior to the mill there was the grinding stone, a nearly universal activity for agrarian societies. As we grind, we sing; we allow the sacred seed to become something more, its essence changed into what it was not before.

CWEORTH takes us before the Goddess whole and mills us down to our essence to make something new. In the transformation we emerge, honed true.

YR

Yew is the tree of life, tree of death. In the liminal, the between, live we, the monstrosities, the hedge riders, the outlaws, the others. We are many, the transgressors. I have always been other, deviant to expectations, but carry my otherness as a story inside: body nonconforming, sexuality nonconforming, spirituality nonconforming, economically nonconforming; a nonconforming mother, teacher, daughter, partner, worker; other other other other.

I am private, I tell the moon, the sea, my intimates. My othering is invisible—like my work, my illness, my depression, my grief, my community. Othering is not something that can be assumed, but herein lies the spirit: in paradox. To be the other is to transgress, but also to contain allness in a whole. Duality was the breaking, the original wound, part of the wider severing: self from community, self from identity, identity from community, community from earth . . . on and on. Parts are easy to control. Wholeness is wild, chaotic, consuming, wholeness is both each and the other, *eachother*.

Like the yew, life is not death but contains death; death is not life but contains life. The yew ignores attempts at containment. Listen: that is the sound of a root inside you. May it grow true.

IOR

"She too is a force of Nature . . . She originally typifies the idea of life emerging from Death and of Death being only a transformation of life."
—commentary on the goddess Hel by Karl Blind in *Yggdrasil, the Teutonic Tree of Existence* written in 1877

IOR is the both. I am the both: dark and light, life and death, day and night. I once thought the task was to choose, to brand, to be carefully slotted into a category. Categories are easy, digestible. But categories separate, and the more categorical I tried to be—mother, professor, consultant, writer, partner, positive, negative, realist, spiritual—the more fragmented I became. And here's why: we are the all, every moment. We cycle, we breathe, we wax and wane. But it is not the dark that comes and goes. The shadow is constant: dark earth, dark space. Light is cyclic; even our sun is burning toward darkness. Dark is beginning and end. What changes when we stop opposing dark and light? What can we claim in the essential both?

Hel is a goddess I work with often. She teaches me to turn toward rather than away from, to question assumption, to not avoid rot. I look at the carcass in the street. I look at the decay in my life. I'm learning to hold Death close because it is here. Like dark, it is the constant. Life emerges from death. Each transition teaches this more. I'm learning to integrate this intimacy, to stop trying to be only one thing. We are many things. We are.

EAR

This rune of the grave speaks to a different kind of transformation, no effort involved. All outside influence is involved in rot. As a corpse transforms over six weeks into soil, so EAR takes its time to reduce—but not a long time. There is no embalming, no protracted decay. It is an allowance, the work of many beings and creatures: bacteria, beetles, fox teeth, and bear claw. The essence of the thing is gnawed away, and what remains is bone.

EAR will leave the bones. They too will dissolve in time, but depending on the constitution of the soil, it may be a long process, even lifetimes. Whatever situation calls EAR into being is one that is certain death, certain decay, contributing to the fertility of whatever comes next. Yet the bones remain to remind us of what was. We are all in EAR a gathering of bone.

OS

The next incarnation is another lightning arm raised, reverence to the gods.

An estuary, river mouth, salty spring and sweetly sexual, OS remembers Freyja as hag, from the German word for witch, *Hexe*, from an old Germanic root meaning "hedge," representing the witch as boundary crosser. Freyja in OS is the Völva, the diviner. Freyja in OS is the psychopomp, as receiver of the dead, a shape-shifter in her falcon cloak, edge walker, rune talker, mixing of the waters.

Freyja is the *hexe*, whose name means "Lady." Writing in thirteenth-century Iceland, Snorri Sturluson said, "She alone of the gods yet lived." Goddess of fertility, abundance, prosperity, deity of the land, of magic and divination, sexuality, autonomy, sovereignty, shapeshifting, from the broken threads, her rich inheritance spans back before written history. Freyja, patron, ancestor, teacher. To her, an offering.

AC

This is the rune of the oak. I grew up in a forest of oak trees, each year witnessing their power in the wind, the tearing of old branches, the steadfast trunks. Oaks scoured by drought survive, oaks adapt to flood, oaks communicate through the mycelium in their roots, live in community, and send each other water and nutrients whenever there is need. Oak is the tree of Druid lore, crown of the Goddess, food of the sacred sow who is Freyja, home of the Hag of the Iron Wood, Myrkwood, Angrboða, mother of the Goddess of Death, the Fenris Wolf, and Jörmundgandr, the World Serpent encircling Midgard. This rune to me is her wisdom, a struck match at the end of time, a sacred task that involves embracing what is monstrous and defying the gods in the process.

So this rune of community, sharing, and nurturance also becomes a rune of outliers, outlaws, hedge riders, edge dwellers. In its lightning arm it holds the all.

OTHALA

This is home, sacred home, sacred space. I chanted OTHALA for moons, sang to it every day, fed it with honey and my blood, this rune of the home that is protection, the space that is enclosure, the ancestral inheritance which is our birthright.

OTHALA so long misused and abused by contemporary culture, called into question as a symbol of other than, OTHALA calls me to home again, singing to the runes. Sound was the beginning of the universe. From this fabric, the wyrd was spun whole. The wyrd is alive: life force, energy, creation, destruction, it forms all that is. From this thread: the runes. Taken up from the Well of Urð, the eldest Norn, the fates or spinners, giantesses at the edge of time, runes are beings. Not merely shapes, not merely an alphabet, not only sigils, not just magic—runes are without an easily identifiable point of origin outside myth. Within the mystery, there grows a possibility of story.

When I create runes, I cut the wood from a single branch of a fruiting tree . . . unless I am feeling untraditional. Sometimes the runes request a specific wood. I lay them in my garden at certain times of year, beneath the plant they attune to. This year I have made runes at the solstice and equinox. I have crafted them from apple, plum, juniper, and hazelwood. They sat beneath mugwort and angelica for full lunar cycles, in sun and wind and rain. When it is time to burn them in the wood, I sing to them.

The runes call to us. They hum in our blood. They fill the marrow of our bones. To study them, to live with them, to craft them, is to me OTHALA, a coming home.

DAGAZ

Movement through the meridian, the labrys axe, cutting away—these are DAGAZ.

I was only five when I began divining with the wind, laying out offerings of blackberries and acorns beneath the oak tree, sitting out at twilight and dawn, watching the change from light to dark, dark to light. Twelve years ago I told the truth and passed a kidney stone aided by strong dandelion vinegar and the sweet meridian pressure of a true friend. That night I dreamed I was in a labyrinth seeking the Minotaur, carrying a labrys high above my head, swinging it down in a figure-eight arc. As it scraped the grey-green stones of the labyrinth sides sparks shot forth.

This is DAGAZ, luminous power, the cutting edge, the shape so ancient it doesn't even have a source, found throughout Old Europe on pottery and bone tool, on megalith and in the tomb. DAGAZ to me is motion and release, the inevitable—unicursal—path of spiritual development and the labyrinthine truth of forward and back simultaneously. DAGAZ is the depth of dark beneath, monstrosities in wait, and also the gentle rise of another day, the blessed dawn, the potency of that knowledge. Life goes on.

I could not ever have envisioned this would be my path. Not as the small child in southern Oregon, not as the single mother who told the truth. DAGAZ teaches me to proceed with trust: in the ancestors, the ancient, always in motion.

INGWAZ

Where are you in the cycle—of death, of birth, of change, of earth?

Yesterday I traveled with INGWAZ to the fertile field and asked this question. I don't normally vision when leading a journey, but immediately I saw scorched earth, the aftermath of the fire cleansing so common in the Willamette Valley where I live. I was at dirt level, eye level, microcosmic, and emerging from the soil, renewal: the tiniest shoots of vibrant green.

In death transitions faith is hard. I've been thinking about these a lot lately, as I sit with mine. What is the difference between a life transition and a death transition? In life transitions, everything carries a modicum of sameness even as you change. Death transitions are wildfire, volcanic, meteoric, or flood. The entire landscape of your life changes. Nothing is recognizable. In the liminal of a life transition you feel still the wyrd webs of support shaping your outcome. In death transition the liminal is dark, chthonic; you are liquid, acid, dust. What happens next is inconsequential. It cannot be visioned—your dissolution is that absolute.

If that sounds bleak, it can be. But death transitions are cyclic, too. Even physical death is not an end in the mythic. I can't speak to all death transitions or even to most. I know intimately that chronic illness is one, and that is why so many people fall away. In death transitions, we become what everyone fears. What nourishes me are the small daily practices, the call to presence, the songs of the runes, the love and prayers of family and friends who remain, even if they are baffled by what they see, even if they don't know how to help.

There is no true help for death transitions, only a way through, only the dance of cycle which is many cycles at once. It is possible to be in life and death transitions simultaneously. Wholeness is nonlinear.

LAGUZ

Learning to flow. Liquid rune.
In a land of water, one rune of water.

This is a feminine essence, but also dark—a lake of leavings, a depth without end. Beginning in the rain, LAGUZ teaches about source wisdom and generosity. Ending in the ocean, LAGUZ teaches about oneness and vastness. In the cycle of evaporation and condensation, LAGUZ teaches that what we cannot see is as real as what we can.

In life, LAGUZ is flow—going with the flow, trusting the process, letting go of expectations.

I have been hoping to improve, and there were a few days where I did feel better, but then I kept crashing.

So hopeful, wishing, I've been waking in the night anxious about my energy, about the realities of my body, and reluctant to take on anything again.

LAGUZ teaches depth and flow. Also the hook of resistance when we refuse to let go. Release can be a blessing, even when it's hard, trusting the current, the spirit, the ancestors to guide this wee leaky boat.

MANNAZ

I meet my ancestors in the between, the tensioning of self-story-myth-root, the chaff on the table, the oat seed in earth, the scent of mugwort rising heady from the land. I meet my ancestors in the matrix of cell and loss, the word *dispossession*, the frantic disappearance from land at sea. They are a you. They are a me. Can you feel the depth of that grief?

I meet my ancestors in language that trips on my tongue—so old I cannot help but remember, so new I can't even pronounce. In the dark of the circle, in the light of no moon, in the alone that is never alone, they wait by the fire. I meet my ancestors in body, embodied, in rhythm, in the animist liminality of between breath. In spiritus, inspiration, ex-hale, ex-ducere, education.

The mycelium spread of what it means to be extends exponentially, MANNAZ the muddle of between, of meaning, of shift and transformation, of protection and communion, of portal and exploration.

I meet my ancestors through his-story, her-story, their-stories, luminous on the cave walls, crawling through the muck of high-minded ideals and precarious theory, backed into the rut of so-called, ever-present truth. They link hands, singing. We wake, if ever, only, singing. The ancestors, singing us to remember their name.

EHWAZ

The horse rune, EHWAZ is LAGUZ facing, evokes twinned flow, rhythm, partnership, the yoke, the goddesses Nerthus and Epona, ritual, sovereignty. From Tacitus's *Germania*, written in 98 CE, an ethnographic treatise on the Germanic tribes: "They share a common worship of Nerthus, or Mother Earth. They believe that she takes part in human affairs, riding in a chariot among her people. On an island of the sea stands an inviolate grove, in which, veiled with a cloth, is a chariot that none but the priest may touch. The priest can feel the presence of the goddess in this holy of holies, and attends her with deepest reverence as her chariot is drawn along by cows."

EHWAZ speaks to the motion that is ritual, the ceremonial in rhythm, the oneness with a companion, human, animal, the secret face of venerated ancestral figures, the cave walls covered in horses. Look in dreams: Nerthus appears, the wagon drawn by cows, shielded and veiled, infused with the fertile, life force too brilliant to see. Look in history: the value of partnership, the cooperative harness of horsepower and strength, the dependency of true relationship.

There is a favorite photo of me as a child, lying on the back of my horse as I did every day after school—often we'd go riding, sure, through the wild rural woods of our shared home. But mostly I just wanted to be near her. The flick of her tail on my legs, soft blow of air through her nostrils, velvet muzzle nibbling, the way she would call for me when she would see me appear, stamping her feet with excitement. On her back I would tell stories and sing songs, and she would pick her way through the forest or down to the creek, often unbridled, the slightest touch of my leg was enough to let her know my wishes. And she had her ways of letting me know hers. It was reciprocal, our bond, and I remember it now with a vividness few human connections from that time retain. I keep a lock of her mane on my altar, remember her every time EHWAZ appears: this magic is possible, this communion real.

Reading the remembering of an oral tradition is like drawing with invisible ink. The patterns are there, but once the ink dries, I cannot recall the shape, and must return again and again. Today I invite EHWAZ in as both chariot and horse to journey these shapes, deep into the mysteries of what was, two thousand years ago, the common. Seeking source in the inviolate grove, drinking from the sacred well.

BERKANA

Mother rune, birth rune, birch rune, poplar rune, breasts of the mother, rune of the labor, rune of the surviving child, rune of the sacred dead in childbed or birth—BERKANA is gentle and savage. She is the cycle; she is the sacred mother of all. Most sources point to BERKANA as soft only, a sweetness like the sap of birch. She presents to me as one of the most challenging runes, as our relationship with the mother is so distant, our birthing practices so tangled in patriarchy, our desire to stay clear of death so present in the sanitization of natural processes.

In contemporary culture we tend to rely on others to receive divine information. Our quests are filtered through teachers, experts. We forget that our ancestors lived their spiritualities and everyone had access to a direct relationship with spirits of the land, animals, ancestors, goddesses, and gods. Awakening our gnosis, following the threads of information on our own research paths, and testing that gnosis through investigation, inquiry, and community return us to an aspect of ancient wisdom. It is in you, already.

This isn't to say that books, guides, teachers aren't helpful—I've found all to be hugely beneficial in rooting my gnosis, reminding me to trust. But they all are interpretive. The lineage traditions for these lifeways and beings were broken by force. In our attention, we repair the wyrd. Recognizing what is true for you, making offerings, ritualizing relationship will bring an accord to whatever other wisdom you encounter. We cannot think our way into knowledge of the runes. We must feel our wholeness and begin again.

You are a part of the weaving, already. The wyrd is woven both forward and back: "Gǽð ā Wyrd swā hīo scel (Wyrd goes ever as it must)," says Beowulf.

The runes whisper: trust, trust, trust.

TYR

Tyr

Tiw

Tuesday

An arrow ascending in my heart, reminder of sacrifice and betrayal—how cued we are in the human condition to the elements of relationship. Tyr is the god who betrayed the Fenris wolf, the fen dweller, the child of Angrboða, brother of the goddess Hel. He paid for that betrayal with his hand, but even that was not enough to forestall fate. Eventually in the myth cycle, Fenris has his vengeance.

There is a directive in the myth cycle, that loss and grief and anger can be a potent death. And death is an essential ingredient in initiation, in transformation, in the full awakening to the soul's purpose. We can choose to see our sacrifice as willing and essential. By this way, a path opens through the forest of unknown.

Our naming of weekdays invoke the Germanic gods and goddesses, an echo of ancient mysteries when the central rhythm of life was divinity. Tyr's name is also Tiw, and his name day became Tiw's Day.

TYR asks where have I been untrue. TYR points the way, takes aim, holds valorous intent. TYR is the scope of wound, the missing piece, the part of the self that is consumed.

In courage, we may heal our wounds. We may cycle through death, ascend to the Mountain of Healing, home of Menglöð, "Necklace of Embers" the healer, and her maidens—named Shelter, Fighting Protection, People Vow, Help, Fair, Friendliness, Pacifying, Healing Goddess, and Moist Earth Offering—where we may be cured of illness, and this completes the cycle, yesterday, today, tomorrow.

SOWILO

This rune calls forth an invocation to the sun, hands raised, arms praising. In the far north the sun is often gendered feminine, a goddess—Sunna, Sol— and her cycles are the necessity of survival, not just a luxury but essential. In this week's Wild Soul Gnosis Group we traveled to the time of ice sheet and migratory mystery, the deep ancestral memory of a two-season landscape, a culture of bone kindred hallowed by cold. In the mystery web of our DNA is memory, recognition, of a cocreative, reciprocal relationship with the sun.

I have never been more dependent on the blessings of the sun. With each day of rain and cold the mold in this house releases more toxins, and my body, unable to get rid of them, exhibits more symptoms. If only the world would dry, I think, I could heal—but that is a distanced perspective. In a cocreative, reciprocal relationship I have to ask what this synergy is saying. I pray and make offerings. And today it is clear: the directive is sanctuary, to find a place to heal, and I can't wait for my husband's new job or my family to move. My body, this time, the clouds, the mold, the wet, the lack of sun—all are urging immediate transformation. The hows and wheres are negligible. I have to ask and act, trusting in the dense weaving of the Norns, the sacred spin of all that is.

One of the great gifts of remembering my ancestors is knowing they survived. My motherline, my haplogroup, is 20,000 years old, originating in the South of France and traveling north along retreating ice. My particular cellular signature is most commonly found in Ireland, with 61 percent of the population coming from the same deep ancestral mother. She survived the ice, the melting, the floods, the fevers; she rejoiced at the turning of the year, the migrations, the soul return of the swans and geese from the water lands of the south. We are one—one in survival, the scrape of it, the trust, the determination, the sheer will. We raise our arms to greet the sun.

ALGIZ

ELHAZ. EOLH SECG. Ancient one, antlered one, food of the four-legged gods, blood of skin, sacrifice in the marshes, perceptive shifts—are you defending, are you defended?

Yesterday's journey with ALGIZ held me with this rune of the elk, elk-sedge, eelgrass, moose. Surrender is my word, and in drawing ALGIZ I felt the container emerge, a holding place, an enclosure of breath and spaciousness. I've had to pull back to essentials, and the rune says, "Show up, I'm here, deepen in, no fear."

ALGIZ reminds me of initiation, of being cut to ribbon flesh by the edges of grasses—those common painful elements of life—then being reassembled in the place of water, of birth, the marshlands, the fen, by the tender hands of a mother, the mother, our fylgia, our Nornir. Before this emergence comes dissolution. ALGIZ creates a cradle, a pen, to hold us together so we can ritually dissolve what no longer is to become what will be. In this moment, we find completion, perfection, *algerr*, free.

PERTHO

This rune is the sacred pouch, grandmother, ancestral womb of my womb of my daughter's womb, prayer to the Nornir, prayer to the Dísir, prayer to the well. At the turning we witches throw the bones, open our cells, and listen. Sometimes the information lands in our bodies; sometimes we are driven to distraction or pain; sometimes we call your name, PERTHO, of uncertain origin, again, again.

But isn't that an untrue gamble? The trickster's laugh? For in crisis we find the calling and the key, the symbols of the path open up and set us free. PERTHO, you are the game and the player, the container and the contents, the shape and the sigil, the design, the dance. Breathing into conscious form the unknown, we light the altar candles, birthing ourselves.

EIHWAZ

The turning, of life and death both, a spirit sense—the moment can change at any time. What was once the underworld becomes the upper world, and the reverse is also true. This, EIHWAZ, I have learned from you.

Gnosis work has changed my life. The idea that I can receive direct spiritual information has revolutionized my receptivity and reciprocity with the world around me. Allowing my gnosis to lead has made me an artist and an integrative listener, but it has also expanded my natural academic longings. As EIHWAZ spoke today, the information coming forward is a thread, a seed, a spark... with research we can follow the thread of knowing into the deeper weaving where pattern emerges, where strength blooms.

EIHWAZ allows for the fullness of above and below. It is the root and the anchor, the air and the bow.

JERA

The feeling of flow is the knowing of the wheel—when to work, when to rest. Illness changes the flow, makes it ever sputtering and not at all consistent. But in attention to the rhythms of nature, there is a story of this dance: do not push, do not crash, pause where needed. Plant while the ground turns, reap while the sun is hot. In the wax and wane of season and moon, there is a path. In the varieties of expectation, there is a lesson.

This week with JERA I have been dreaming of work with an open heart. Trusting in the timing, knowing in my bones the effort required for planting, harvest, and rest.

When JERA speaks to me, it is always as a feminine earthen being, a spirit of the grain, grown and waving, cut with a scythe, stacked in the corners for the beings of the stable. JERA is our collective harvest, our memory of cycle time, and the belief in relationship of earth-self-plant-moon-sun-star-kin.

May the path be open.

May the balance be regained.

ISA

Yesterday in meditation I realized that like so many runes, ISA—the rune of manifestation—contains multitudes, simultaneously of stillness and motion. Rune of the ice mystery, its singularity is a clear conduit, a container for honing and channeling information. Through the portals of its crystalline form, all can be transmuted and channeled the way light travels through a portal. ISA centers energy—like calcite, like cables, like the magical pulses through the conduits of nerves. Suddenly, what I thought of as stillness was actually a channel, with new information pouring through.

As I write this, I wrap my grandmother's shawl a little closer around me. This is a big week of undoing old patterns, invoking new information. Later today I'll be making a dark moon ritual with one of my favorite practices for untangling the old and invoking the new—simultaneously.

I am ever amazed at the revelations of these beings. Blessings to ISA for opening the portals, for clarity, for what pours through.

NAUDHIZ

A Prayer
Friction. Need. Needfire.
NAUDHIZ, you are my trouble rune.
I gain trouble by refusing you.
You say need is but a word for effort.
Whittle short the fire stick, make it little, make it thick.
Round it with your tinder fine
cross your leg then under mine.
The hearth fire does not build itself.
The bow drill does not twirl alone.
The sacred rub of sex is peril

The heat reductive, flesh to bone.
You are not fear. It is my fear I hold at the center,
dreaming in ridicule of all I require.
NAUDHIZ, you say, survive.
You say, come:
build your fire.

HAGALAZ

I first dreamed of Hel, venerated mythic figure, ancestor, keeper of the Dead, creatrix, regenerator, stroking my hair with her bone hand. She is half dead, half living, and my head rested on her bone knee, her hand a gentle scraping. It was deeply peaceful, I was unafraid.

And that year, the year I began working with the runes, her rune—for that is how I think of HAGALAZ—appeared no less than nine times in the twenty-six full and dark moons of my annual rune wheel reading.

It might be the wrong number, nine, for I no longer have that journal or wheel, but nine feels right for the charge of HAGALAZ through my life. And so that year was: chaos, upended, homes lost, children displaced, transitions, trials, and more. And yet, when it ended, the way was clear, what was maligned became aligned, and I found a deep wisdom and power in facing the uncomfortable, necessary story. HAGALAZ, stormbringer, is kin to me, sister through the Myrkwood witch Angrboða, Hel's mother, and a lineage of shape-shifters. I barely know her in this life, yet she knows me well and full.

In working with the runes, I've found the blessing of my fear and the presence of my ancestors, the workings of wyrd no less mysterious but true. These song beings, these sound forms, these drum an aspect that calls us in. Listen listen, we are kin.

WUNJO

JOY and Reclaiming our Birthright
WUNJO Plants and the Mountain of Healing

This week I sat in circle community to practice healing the witch wound. For this moon's topic we explored embodied, ancestral wisdom, reading selections from the penitentials—books written by priests to "correct" the folk practices and pagan-heathen beliefs of the common people . . . many were focused on women. Thank the ancestors for the penitientials, for without them so much wisdom would have been lost. In combing through prohibitions we find divination, herbal wisdom, nature worship, love spells, funerary rites, and so much more. We can also find the insidious threads demanding control of bodies, sexuality, fertility, spirituality, parenting, community, celebration, and agency. In short, the groundwork is clearly being laid for the systemic oppressions still in place today.

When we travel back far enough in our lineages, we are all somewhere people of the earth, people of the moon and sun cycles, people of the waterways, people of plants and ceremonies, people of magic. Layered over this fundamental knowing are centuries of fear. When I first began to journey into the worlds of nonhuman beings, of ancestors, the intensity of welcome I felt was overwhelming—and terrifying. In one of my lineage traditions the goddess Menglo∂ lives on the Mountain of Healing, and any woman who seeks healing may come to her for help. I have drawn her with the Nine Sacred Herbs of the Anglo-Saxons, as they appear in the Lacnunga manuscript. She has helped me many times on this journey to wholeness, to be strong and surrendering both, to proceed unafraid knowing millions of ancestors stand around me, holding sacred my task, aiding in my healing of ancient wounds.

WUNJO is the joy of healing, whose root word means wholeness. WUNJO is the medicine of the plants, the song of galdr that is an offering, the reweaving of ancestral lifeways. This healing of WUNJO belongs to us all. Not just some of us, not just a faction or group or special people. Some of us have older wounds, some newer; the road is individuated but healing is ours for all.

GEBO

The gift is the sacrifice. The sacrifice is the gift. GEBO to me is the guardian of transition, the give-and-take that happens when we are in the liminal.

In this time of change I reach into roots, finding gathered at the well of remembrance a host of helpers. The guides and guardians wear ancient names: Fylgjur, Dísir, Nornir.

In the overlap of the mythic, we are cared for by the *fylgja*, a word that means "follower," a spirit that cares for us through our cycles. They may be ancestral mothers, related to the Dísir and the Norns. They may also take the shape of animals offering counsel, protect us from danger, and defend against enemies. In modern scientific methodologies we seek to neatly categorize the spirits, but my intuition cautions against this, urging us to embrace a more fluid cosmology of overlap between goddesses, ancestors, nature spirits, to embrace the indistinct.

The theme through all, river and source, is communion and protection. Seen or unseen, acknowledged or ignored, the spirits are here. We have only to remember.

We are not alone in this journey. None of us ever were.

KENNAZ

KENNAZ is the one rune I truly feel as a fire rune as a wedge of illumination presented on the axis. Shifting perspective transformed my relationship with the runes. When I ceased to view them as one-dimensional shapes, symbols, or alphabets and began to see them as beings, the movement was astounding. I am still surprised every time I draw them, because it is not ever me drawing them. It is them, coming through. This is KENNAZ.

I also see KENNAZ as the rune of art, illuminating the cave. Making art has taken a back seat in the past few months of transition. Family has come first, along with health. I still don't have a work space where I can leave my art out—key for any artist with limited energy . . . when the art is out, I can draw a line or two here or there. But working at the kitchen table with weeks of people home with illness—with weeks of me unwell—has been a nonstarter. Last year at this time, with these issues, I started painting. I invested in brushes, canvas, and enough paints to splash around in color. Making intricate portraits became quickly out of the question, but painting the runes was a revelation: a less physically intensive mode of expression. (The line art I do is meditative but often very hard on my body.) With the mold infestation in our home, everything had to go, including those new paints and brushes, the canvases, the art . . . though I feel a pattern in the cycles of the year, the call to paint again in this season of virus and wet.

KENNAZ invites a knowing, even through pain. It asks for the burn to be a wholeness, the creation to be a sacrifice. It offers the bright wisdom we don't always seek (don't show me!) but are inevitably grateful to know.

RAIDO

This week I moved in mythic time. The warp was caused by a virus—so many viruses!—traveling through my family over the past weeks. The immune system is beautifully complex, and in someone compromised or poisoned by toxins or stress, viruses can cause surreal reactions.

My virus experiences never look like my family's anymore, being often coupled with extreme fatigue, vivid dreams, and changes in perception and ability—including things we take for granted: the ability to string words together, the ability to recall information, the ability to see a situation in clarity. It is disorienting, difficult to tell what is going on: Is this the virus? Is this emotional? Is this a toxic reaction, distress, overwhelming? All is skewed. The only solution is rest and nourishment, and only time will tell whether these distortions are in resolution or chronic. Today it came clear, I finally have the cold that made its way through everyone else. But it has taken nearly two weeks to manifest, and in the meantime I have traveled on a road I know too well: the winter road, dark and bare. It's the one where I spend hours each day watching the clouds move, the trees bend, where I dream in prophecy and shake on waking.

RAIDO is the rune of the journey. It is the first rune I ever pulled. It can be a physical journey, but it is also the visionary journey, the spiritual journey. RAIDO invites the nonlinear. Every time I try to straighten up, get on track, get my act together, move into linearity, I am drawn back into the journey of cycle. Tidal, menstrual, earthen, RAIDO asks me to rest in the depths, to not know, to be rhythmic, to trust the teaching however uncomfortable. Again, again, again, and never the same.

ANSUZ

Exploring through the runes in a way open and undefined by expectation allows for feeling. While ANSUZ is classically considered a masculine rune, it whispers shapes of the feminine. In exploring the cosmology of the north, the qualities of masculine and feminine—present in all—are necessary components in the powerful force of creation.

The masculine acts as a visible holding, seen and known, where the feminine is unseen and unknown, free.

It is difficult to extract a brain from the binary, gendered, patriarchal matrix we inhabit, to allow for the interplay, the magic of the both. The most beautiful reframings are happening though, in this and other spaces. As I enter the fourth week with the runes in meditation, I invite the possibilities of their many worlds, beyond this one. I open perception and eternally begin, calling on the guardians, to ANSUZ, to the ancestors, in offering.

THURISAZ

What the ancestors knew: animism, spirit-centered, both/and, healing, medicine, metaphysics, science, politics, poetry, metaphor, the shape of the world, the beginning of time, navigation, making of all things from nature, returning all things to nature, gender spectrums, equality, power, reverence, reciprocity, the necessity of chaos, cycle, simultaneous thought, real/not-real, nonbinary, death as an aspect of life, life as an aspect of death, blood mysteries, honor, truth telling, storytelling . . . and on and on and on—these are THURISAZ.

This week's runic meditation is taking me into the realm of the giants, whose cosmic importance in the mythic is, well, gigantic. It is also making me think of words and how retraining our brains to remember the ancestors, to attempt to see through their eyes, opens us to the possibility that everything we've learned is a story told through the lens of forgetting.

I opened this entry with a partial list of forgotten things. There are so many. Recently colonized cultures can complete the list in thousands, millions, of details and legacy passed from generation to generation for millennia lost or shredded by the imposition of oppressive religious and cultural norms that would not allow for anything other. Cultures of the colonizers are far from the process of forgetting, so the lists are relegated to a quaint past and bare . . . until one begins looking in earnest for what was forgotten. It is all still there, torn, but present. As I pull on the threads of the giants in a mythos ancient,

I feel the emergence of memory, like a net rising from the sea. Only a few things are visible, but the weight indicates a lifetime of pulling in.

The Old World: Old. Old ways, old thoughts, old memories, old beings. Old food, old drink, old craft, old art, old languages, old spirits entering our dreams, inviting us into the realms of the round, the continuous, the spiral, the sacred. *Old* comes from the word *ald* (Anglian), *eald* (West Saxon) for "aged, antique, primeval; elder, experienced"; from Proto-Germanic *althaz*, "grown up, adult," originally a stem of a verb meaning "grow, nourish" (compare to Old Norse *ala* "to nourish").[43]

The old nourishes us. It grows us up. The old/auld sings in the year with fire and calls by its name the drums and pipes of remembering.

URUZ

URUZ, the rune of this week's runic journey, helps me remember the old. It tastes of ice strength and carries hope in its power. URUZ is a name for the aurochs, the enormous wild ox of Europe that stood larger than a man in height. Their strength, stamina, and untamed nature made them desirable and dangerous.

As I press into the land of healing, I think of the lessons inherent in URUZ— that wild species are always heartier than tame, due to food and exercise, fresh air, sunshine, and a resilience born of isolation. What does this hold for our physical being? The word URUZ makes me long for fresh greens, like Rapunzel's mother craving the rampion in the witch's garden. The air here blows fierce, and I imagine a Europe of old that could nourish herds of URUZ. Their genes live still in a carefully managed species of European bison, forest dwelling now, hidden from sight.

What happens when we reclaim the wildness of URUZ? Is it even possible in this day to harness an energy hunted to extinction? What would be the equivalent genetically here in the United States? Is there a kind of huge wildness that we can reclaim in the wyrd?

FEHU and Elder Languages

This week began the journey of the runes, and it is so potent to hear the stories of travelers on this path. I'm caught in the brain balance of wanting to offer everything—the tons of research and information, all I can find—and resting in the reality that this is a journey, with each person accountable to their own relationships. The runes are beings, and building affinity in all relationships comes with time.

This said, I realized that the rune poems have been a help in my dissolving meaning and opening to the figurative language of the ancestors, seeing the range, feeling into the impossibility of translation, allowing the images to feed imagining. The runes speak a language beyond language, the elder of all rhythms. When we seek them, we seek beyond speaking into a realm of shape, sound, sense.

FEHU is wealth but built from relationship. When I first encountered FEHU, I saw a rune card with the image of a cow on it and realized that the definition of material wealth for my ancestors was very different from our contemporary accumulation of real or imaginary coin and goods. Wealth as defined by cattle is wealth tended—a mortal wealth with interspecies interdependence at its core. I remember watching an episode of the PBS show *Frontier House* many years ago where the historian said finding a milk cow in this day and age was next to impossible: the people who raised milk cows were very attached to them and did not wish to be apart from them or loan them out. This concept of wealth as something living, which must be nurtured, loved, and interacted with daily is a potent clue to the meaning of FEHU. It is not about selfish accumulation, hoarding, or consumption. It is about giving and receiving.

Runes and Ceremonial Divination

Veiztu hvé rísta skal?
Veiztu hvé ráða skal?
Veiztu hvé fá skal?
Veiztu hvé freista skal?
Veiztu hvé biðja skal?
Veiztu hvé blóta skal?
Veiztu hvé senda skal?
Veiztu hvé sóa skal?
From the Hávámal, Sayings of the High One, or Odin, in the Poetic Edda
referring to the processes with the runes.

My translation:
Do you know how to cut (skal)?
Do you know how to advise (skal)?
Do you know how to draw (skal)?
Do you know how to tempt (skal)?
Do you know how to wait (skal)?
Do you know how to curse (skal)?
Do you know how to send (skal)?
Do you know how to destroy (skal)?

The word *skal* in Old Icelandic means "bowl/cup/skull" and is the root of the toast *skoal*, "cheers, to your health." It is presumed to come from the ancient tradition of toasting with the skulls of your enemies. Here it is perhaps seen as an affirmation or ritual blessing, a raising of the cup.

We know from ancient written sources that runes were used for divination, magic, and imbuing objects with power. Much of our understanding of how the runes were interacted with comes from conjecture. For example, in the observations of Tacitus regarding the Germanic tribes, he writes: "For omens and the casting of lots they have the highest regard. Their procedure in casting lots is always the same. They cut off a branch of a nut-bearing tree and slice it into strips; these they mark with different signs and throw them completely at random onto a white cloth. "[44] From the Poetic Edda to the Sagas we see runes used to empower objects and divine the future, but little concrete instruction remains—as Oðin's riddle above indicates, the question is, do you know?

So many of the books on runes profess to tell how to divine with them. At the beginning of this one I asked for a consideration—that the runes were beings, and in a sentient, animate universe, deserving of an approach to relationship. Rushing to divination before even properly introducing yourself is like having sex before knowing someone's name: maybe great for a one-night stand, but could have far-reaching consequences. Most relationships are built on time, communication, effort, and intention. To work with the runes is to allow for a dismantling of industrial, capitalist, colonial mentality by making a slow way into relationship.

Once you have developed a relationship with the runes, asking them how they wish to be read is the first step. Then you have to *listen* for their answer—it may not be immediate; it might never be affirmative. Preparing to receive information from the runes prior to reading them will support a positive outcome whatever path you take.

I worked deeply with the runes for five years, and in the beginning I was not "allowed" to use the runes for divination. I felt this as a strong internal prohibition. I was in a state of apprenticeship and transformation and was not ready to engage them in reading the wyrd—yet.

Instead, I sat with them in classes, read about them in books, began making altars and working in relationship with them. I was allowed to experience rune readings from other people, though only for a few years. My breakthrough began when I started drawing rune art. Art became my portal into gnosis, the divine information speaking directly from the runes. First, I drew them individually, then placed them on the axis—which was the determining moment for me. Setting the runes on a diagonal gave them a fractal sensation. The mysteries of the Norse myths came to light: a story of ice and fire, the web of wyrd fragmented in the well of the Norns. Soon I was drawing webs of wyrd from rune casts on sacred days, but I was still not allowed to interpret them.

I had to undergo a huge life transition, a ritual death, before I was allowed to divine wyrd with the runes.

My path will not be yours, and I share my divination method here as I share all in this book: not as a proscription but as a journey.

Runes are ancient beings. They are not for entertainment, not a parlor trick, not a game. To work with them is to transform your life, to divine with them is to offer yourself in partnership. As Oðin asks in the *Hávamál*, "Do you know how to tempt (skal)?" This is a collaborative prayer, a willing sacrifice, of your time, attention, and preconception for a glimpse of the wyrd. It is a fair exchange.

Rune Webs and Reading the Wyrd

As an artist I discovered my own path to casting the runes and interacting with them through sacred art. I have found this process to be particularly effective for gaining a snapshot of wyrd over a lunar or solar cycle. I call these creations *rune webs*, custom works of art crafted in ritual for the purpose of making wyrd visible.

Wyrd is only one aspect of fate. There is also ørlög to consider. If we think of the web of fate as a weaving, ørlög is the weft strands, laid on the loom by our ancestors and all that came before us. Ørlög is fortune, fate, largely unchangeable. Some parts of a rune web, however many times runes are cast and the art made, are unchanging. Ørlög deserves notice and attention, for it informs our wyrd. Wyrd is changeable, moving always, so rune webs can be a way to synthesize these two perspectives of fate.

I share my process here as one of many ways to take your personal strength and apply it to rune practice. Because drawing, painting, and carving are so much a part of rune lore, my skills as an artist held a natural affinity for them. Seeking in the primary sources and with the runes themselves for your own way into divination will ultimately lead you to the path of gnosis: that synthesis of ancient wisdom and contemporary application that is all your own.

Ritual for Rune Web Reading

Readings include a ritual rune cast, a process for crafting a custom black-and-white hand-drawn web of wyrd from the cast runes and some notes on interpretation.

Supplies for the ritual:

- Pens and paper
- A white cloth

- A set of runes

- A candle or other source of nonelectric light

- Mead or other drink for offering

- Ancestral objects or photos nearby

- Three small knives to represent the Nornir

- A platter with bread, nuts, and fruit

1. Choose a lunar-solar cycle that has resonance with you. This can be a full or dark moon, a time of day or the week—whatever you feel called to share. I like to work readings on the holy days of the Anglo-Saxon and Germanic wheel or at the potent moon times, but this is another place of listening to what your ancestors and the runes ask of you.

2. Consider your intention for the rune cast. Craft a question. This should not be a yes or no question, but one where you seek a picture, a path. If you have difficulty holding the question in mind, write it down and keep it in a safe place. The night before the rune cast I like to keep my question under my pillow so that I can dream on it.

3. Set aside time and space where you won't be interrupted. Spread out the white cloth and make a small altar with space for your ancestral objects, runes, and offerings. Begin by breathing to center yourself. I like to imagine I am a tree, breathing down into my roots and up into my branches. Light your candle to begin the ritual. I like to imagine a protective circle around my ritual space, orienting myself to the cardinal directions and above/below, seeing myself in a sphere of wyrd—a web or light.

4. Once grounded and centered I usually call in the Dísir from any lineage I am reading for, as they are supportive of wyrd shaping. I also call in the Nornir, and in this ritual you acknowledge them with their three knives, an ancient representation of these wyrd sisters. If you feel so moved, you can cut off pieces of your offering and host them

for a moment, lifting your cup in a ritual sip or pouring some drops out onto your hearth, altar, or the earth.

5. Invite in the runes. You have developed a relationship with them, so call them by name, sing to them, or simply speak to them with your mind. You are asking for aid and assistance, not demanding. If it feels like they don't want to help, don't force it. Timing is important, as are your feelings. When ready, focus on your question and reach your hand into the runes. What happens next is up to you. I sometimes draw one rune at a time or a handful, casting the runes on white linen. The order of the runes cast and relationship between the runes are both important in my readings, so I keep a record of this when I conclude the ritual.

6. You may choose to begin your art in the ritual casting or work with it over time. My process is the latter. I close the circle in ritual, honoring all of the ancestors, Dísir, Nornir, directions and protectors, and, of course, the runes. I place all of the food and drink outside with a blessing, and sit with the results of the reading . . . sometimes for days. Then I start drawing. As I draw the runes together, they begin to form other runes, and a full picture emerges. The initial handmade rune web takes me one to two weeks to complete. Once I finish the web, I like to spend time with it for a while before I endeavor to begin the reading, so I usually put it on my altar or in a place where I can look at it both peripherally and directly, noticing what is revealed.

This process may be repeated as a regular rhythm. I now regularly craft rune webs for myself, others, in independent readings, as rituals, and for groups. The more I deepen into this unique form of divinatory practice, the more I begin to understand the wyrd, how it shapes, and the influences of these beings in it. I like to imagine this impacts my ørlög, as the subtle shapes on the woof affect the warp threads of the loom—strong weaving, a legacy, across the span of mythic time.

Closing the Practice: Sharing Your Gnosis

We are all made to receive divine information. As you have journeyed through this book, you have opened yourself to the ancestral wisdom of this earth, the elements, and the beings and creatures that came before. You have perhaps begun to remember that you are made of ancestors, human and nonhuman—all of the information encoded in their survival and adaptation lives within you. Maybe you have discovered resonance with the web of wyrd, the strands of fate that led you to this process, and are even now weaving with me this new and ancient story of reconnected honoring.

But how can you know your gnosis experience is real?

How can you close this practice and yet continue, taking this information into your larger life and continuing to allow the spirit threads to transform the pattern of your existence?

I am by nature a solitary practitioner, but what I have found is that sharing my practice through gathering and writing has been vital to affirming and growing my gnosis.

The practice of the wyrd path never ends. It is, like myth and ancestral time, intended to be cyclic and nonlinear.

As each cycle closes, another opens.

With each round is an opportunity to invite others in.

This week I begin another season of The Wild Soul Gnosis Group. My brain injury and medical limitations prevent me from hosting live, in-person classes, but this online gathering has been a wonderful addition to my gnosis practice. We work independently with the runes each week, then gather at the end of the week's practice to share our gnosis.

What comes through is affirming—overlap, opening, sustaining, and expansive.

This is yours as well: the possibility of sharing the process with friends, family, children, community to deepen relationship, to grow the journey, to make this work an offering to the Nornir and all of our ancestors.

When we gather to listen to the whispers of the runes, we join a reciprocal imagining. And they listen too, waiting for our intention.

Þaðan koma meyjar margs vitandi
þrjár, ór þeim sal er und þolli stendr;
Urð hétu eina, aðra Verðandi,
skáru á skíði, Skuld ina þriðju;
þær lög lögðu, þær líf kuru
alda börnum, örlög seggja.[45]

Then come maidens many knowing
Three out of the hall that under tree stands
Origin (Urð) is called one, another To Happen (Verðandi)
They cut in wood—Debt (Skuld) is third.
They laws laid, they lives chose.
Lifetimes children, fate to tell.

—From the *Völuspá*, my translation

May your Dísir be honored. May your wyrd weave powerful and free. May the Nornir, in their wisdom, carve well upon the Tree.
With love.

Appendix A

Timeline of the Runes

This timeline contains archaeological and/or written source materials regarding the runes. (for reference only, not comprehensive. All dates are approximate.)

7000–3000 BCE: The period of Maria Gimbutas's Old European civilization

6000–5000 BCE: The Old European Sacred Script is in wide use.

3180–2100 BCE: Proto-writing of Skara Brae, Orkney, Scotland

3000 BCE: Orkney Venus figurine, oldest Neolithic human figure found in Northern Europe.

50 CE: The Meldorf fibulae from Meldorf, Germany, with runic, proto-runic, or Latin characters. If runic, it would be the oldest example of runic inscription found.

98 CE: The Roman writer Tacitus publishes *Germania*, a history of the Germanic peoples that references a form of divination thought to refer to the runes.

100–700 CE: Elder Futhark inscriptions of twenty-four runes used by the Germanic peoples

160 CE: The Vemose comb, from Denmark, the earliest confirmed rune script artifact

200 CE: The spearhead of Kovel, Ukraine, providing evidence for the runes in Eastern Europe

400 CE: The Pietrossa Romania rune ring, possibly reads "sacred to the gothic women."

425–475 CE: Caistor-by-Norwich astragalus carving, earliest rune find in England, predates the Anglo-Frisian futhork

500–1000 CE: Anglo-Saxon/Anglo Frisian twenty-nine-rune furhork rune script used in England and Frisia

700 CE: The Franks casket or Auzon casket inscribed with Anglo-Saxon runes and an image of three cloaked women presumed to be the Nornir

700–1200 CE: The Younger Futhark sixteen-rune script used in Scandinavia

800–900 CE: The Abecedarium Nordmannicum rune poem written in sixteen-rune Younger Futhark and a mix of Old Norse, Old Anglo-Saxon, and Old High German. Original was destroyed, surviving copy dates from 1828.

800–900 CE: Old English Rune Poem written in Old Anglo-Saxon, original destroyed in 1731, surviving copy dates 1705

900 CE: Northumbrian Runes: CWEORTH, CALC, STAN, GAR, appear in manuscripts, rings, and crosses bringing the total number of runes to thirty-three.

1200 CE: Medieval rune script emerges, a twenty-seven-letter Scandinavian alphabet adding dotted runes.

1220 CE: The Prose Edda (likely) written by Snorri Sturluson in Iceland. Seven manuscripts survive, none are complete.

1270 CE: The Poetic Edda is compiled from older materials thought to date from 800–1000 CE. It was rediscovered in 1643, and though the original survives, pages are missing.

Appendix B

Rune Resources

The Poetic Edda

Thought to be written in medieval Iceland, shortly after conversion to Christianity, but containing material thought to be much older, the Poetic Edda is the surviving legacy of an oral culture's myths. This translation by Henry Adams Bellows is respected, well footnoted, and in the public domain. There are many translations, and comparison also offers insight, so see what resonates with you. *www.sacred-texts.com*

The Prose Edda

Written in Iceland by Snorri Sturluson around 1200 CE, it is the narrative of myths and interpretations, and it is helpful to explore alongside the Poetic Edda to compare and contrast information. *www.sacred-texts.com*

Taking Up the Runes by Diana Paxson

This is the first book I encountered when studying the runes. It is a comprehensive guide to the twenty-four Elder Futhark runes, including rune poems and lore. Paxson is a scholar and practicing Heathen, so balances the two beautifully. This book was a great introduction and helped me get my bearings with the lore.

The Lady of the Labyrinth

Maria Kvilhaug, religious historian with a foundation in Norse myths and initiation rituals, has compiled a vast and rich repository of stories, facts and resources centered in the feminine. She shares full-text versions of her thesis, *The Maiden and the Mead*, on her website, as well as her essays on many topics relative to Norse mythology. She is the translator of *The Poetic Edda: Six Cosmology Poems*, as well as the wonderful *The Seed of Yggdrasil: Discovering the Hidden Meanings in Old Norse Myths*. Her work inspired me to begin my own translations. *http://freya.theladyofthelabyrinth.com*

Norse Mythology for Smart People

Another great site with definitions and beginnings rooted in fact and text, this resource is worth a visit if you encounter a god, goddess, term, or being that you want to know more about. *https://norse-mythology.org*

Books and Resources for the First Third Reflection

Civilizations of the Goddess by Marija Gimbutas

This book is an archaeological chronicle through Old European civilization prior to the Indo-European invasions. Highly pictoral, the symbolism is very relevant to anyone seeking the runes in history, or seeking ancestral connection.

Jung and the Ancestors: Beyond Biography, Mending the Ancestral Web by Sandra Easter

Easter writes, "Whatever one believes about the existence of the soul after death, these 'ghosts' of memory (trauma) have archetypal weight. I would suggest that when these 'ghosts,' the ancestors, are engaged with consciously, the result is similar to what one experiences when one comes into relationship with any complex—an 'easing of psychic tension,' and an 'undreamed of expansion and enrichment of life.'" She also includes tools for working with the ghosts of our lineage wounds.

Caliban and the Witch: Women, the Body and Primitive Accumulation by Silvia Federici

This is a vital book that connects many of our modern systems of oppression to the rise of capitalism, land privatization, and Christianity in European civilization. All oppressions were internalized in the bodies of women and men during the witch hunts, a time we know little about but which has still imprinted the very patterns of our relationships in personal, political, and spiritual ways. This book takes us through analysis of that time of transformation and illustrates how it paved the way for slavery and the colonization of other countries and cultures—including the Americas. All oppression is connected. More than any other, this book gave me an academic understanding of the overwhelming knot in our collective wyrd. As we begin to untangle these threads, we may find our way back to the time before . . . I highly recommend the whole thing, but if you could only read two chapters, "The Great Witch Hunt in Europe" and "Colonization and Christianization: Caliban and the Witches in the New World" are both incredibly worthwhile. I wish I could scan them and share them with everyone, but they are nearly half the book and well over fair use. This is a worthwhile purchase; I also found it at my local library.

Witches and Pagans: Women in European Folk Religion, 700–1100
by Max Dashú
This book is one of what will be sixteen in a series titled The Secret History of the Witches. Dashú is a scholar of women's mysteries and sacred arts. She runs a website database called Suppressed Histories, which provides comprehensive literature about women's power and spirituality the world over. The pre-Christian world of Europe is often dismissed by academia as "cultish," but Dashú provides excellent evidence of lost practices and fragments of a rich, earth-affirming, life-abundant culture. As we recall what was lost, we can see what may be gained.

Resources on Grief and Grieving

Finnish Lament Singing
Lament singing is found in many cultures as a way to express emotions and clear grief. In Finland there is a resurgence in learning Lament Singing. It survived despite Christian resistance.
www.yesmagazine.org; Tristan Ahtone, "How an Ancient Singing Tradition Helps People Cope with Trauma in the Modern World," May 16, 2017
https://vimeo.com/87757291

How Trauma Is Carried Across Generations
"In rising above the remnants of one's ancestors' trauma, one helps to heal future generations."
www.psychologytoday.com; Molly S. Castelloe, "How Trauma Is Carried Across Generations," May 28, 2012

Resources and Readings for Second Third Reflection

***Ancient Spirit Rising: Reclaiming Your Roots and Restoring Earth Community* by Pegi Eyers**

Eyers's book is specifically for those struggling to understand earth reclaiming in the face of intersectional oppressions or anyone who has participated in cultural/spiritual appropriation consciously or unconsciously. Her blog also has many excellent resources.

Discovering a Sense of Place—Discussion Course Sampler

This is a course I used for years with freshmen at Pacific University. We held weekly "experience days" at B Street Living Museum, a permaculture project and working farm. Last fall my students were the most diverse group yet, racially and culturally, but each had a deep affinity for a place in their past and developed roots in community at the farm. The course is no longer available—though NWEI has a number of other community discussion courses that are wonderful—but this introduction includes a map of continental U.S. ecoregions that I found useful. *www.nwei.org*

Bioregional Quiz

> *Of all the memberships we identify ourselves by (racial, ethnic, sexual, national, class, age, religious, occupational), the one that is most forgotten, and that has the greatest potential for healing, is place. We must learn to know, love, and join our place even more than we love our own ideas. People who can agree that they share a commitment to the landscape/cityscape—even if they are otherwise locked in struggle with each other—have at least one deep thing to share.*
>
> —Gary Snyder

I have taken this quiz every time I move. It builds my awareness about the systems that nourish me and the ancestral skills specific to where I live.

Old School Single Page—downloadable and basic, no ads
https://dces.wisc.edu; Leonard Charles, Jim Dodge, Lynn Milliman, and Victoria Stockley, "Where You At? A Bioregional Quiz," originally printed in *Coevolution Quarterly* 32 (Winter 1981)
New School—Interactive with suggestions, expansions, and advertising
www.patheos.com; Rua Lupa, "Ehoah Bioregional Quiz, How Well Do You Know the Place in Which You Live?" May 31, 2013, *Paths through the Forest* blog

Tribal Nations Map—Prior to Settlement/Colonization/Empire drawn by Aaron Carapella (Cherokee)
http://legacy.npr.org; "Tribal Nations Map"

Last Universal Common Ancestor
This article in the *New York Times* discusses the (controversial) Last Universal Common Ancestor theory of a single-celled progenitor of all life on earth.
www.nytimes.com; Nicholas Wade, "Meet Luca, the Ancestor of All Living Things," July 25, 2016

The Norse Creation Story
This is the song of ice and fire and shows interesting parallels to the origin of the Last Universal Common Ancestor.
https://norse-mythology.org; Daniel McCoy, "The Creation of the Cosmos," accessed November 2020

There are a million directions to travel in connecting with place-based ancestor work. In exploring them for ourselves, we are opening to a lifetime of practice and discovery.

Resources and Reading for Third Reflection

This third's resources explore a variety of methods around ancestral ways of knowing, historical context, Indigenous traditions, ecofeminism, the Eleusinian Mysteries, and reimagining ancestral traditions. The goal of offering such a wide variety of perspectives is to awaken your own curiosity and prime you for further investigation. Again, this is in no way comprehensive.

Cultural Appropriation

A note on cultural appropriation: Learning about contemporary Indigenous cultures and working to support Indigenous peoples is vital. If you are from a culture whose strands are frayed with regard to ancestral ways or memory, there is always a temptation to find ancestors of affinity within a group with more contemporary earth-based lineages and call that practice or to claim the small fragment of ones' lineage connected to Indigenous traditions.

But this limited perspective of what constitutes earth-affirming ancestry also prevents the good and necessary work of healing and reweaving the frayed threads of history. What we explore in the privacy of our own homes is up to us; cultural/spiritual appropriation in its most insidious form involves capitalism—stealing or misusing sacred or cultural practices from cultures you are not a part of then selling them or gaining social profit from them. Research, education, and solidarity work are not cultural appropriation, nor is loving aspects of another's culture. These acts of service and affinity can serve to awaken parts of our spirit to practices from our own lineage. No one should fear investigation, but we should be open to understanding the consequences of cultural/spiritual appropriation and work to prevent it.

Everyday Feminism: What, Exactly, Is Cultural Appropriation and How Is It Harmful?
This great video helped me understand cultural appropriation better. *https://everydayfeminism.com;* Marina Watanabe, "What, Exactly, Is Cultural Appropriation (And How Is It Harmful)?" December 22, 2014

New Age Fraud
This site is a forum investigating cultural appropriators and other New Age frauds and plastic shamans. I have found it helpful in evaluating a number of people as I look into spiritual work and before I make purchases or support projects. It is not definitive, but certainly helps give context. *www.newagefraud.org*

Death Work–Ancestral

The Road to Hel: A Study of the Conception of the Dead in Old Norse Literature by Hilda Roderick Ellis

Ellis explores the funeral rites, ancestral reverence, grave mound customs, and other perceptions of death.

Death Work–Modern

Crossing the Creek: A Practical Guide to Understanding the Dying Process by Michael Holmes

This book written by a hospice nurse helps to normalize and naturalize the process of dying. It is simple, straightforward, and easy to understand. It is also free. *www.crossingthecreek.com*

Take Me Home

There are many beautiful videos of home funerals online. This one follows an elder through the process of planning her own death. Confronting the grief of others can be powerfully cathartic, and watching death, seeing dead bodies, can be painful or healing, but seems at least necessary.

www.youtube.com, "Take Me Home—Home Funeral & Death Midwifery by Sacred Crossings," June 19, 2015, uploaded by Olivia Bareham

Living Ancestral Ways

Not all of these books are from the Norse or Anglo-Saxon tradition—some are from the Gaelic or Slavic—but I have found it useful to compare these various branches in furthering my ancestral remembering.

Carolyn Hillyer

> *What is the story of our forgotten people? It is a story of return. . . . Remembering our people, those who are connected to us by blood or clan or land or any other bond that serves to entwine hearts and souls, is part of rooting ourselves in our landscape and shaping the road along which we choose to travel. We learn from our ancestors in order to understand the ancestors we might become.*
>
> —Carolyn Hillyer

Carolyn Hillyer's ancestor work is deeply experiential, involving crafting a Neolithic round house for ritual, music for honoring, artwork from the depths of her gnosis. *www.seventhwavemusic.co.uk*

The Way of the Wise: Traditional Norwegian Folk and Magic Medicine by J. T. Sibley
A wonderful collection of folklore and wisdom from the healing and magical traditions of Norway.

Healing Threads: Traditional Medicines of the Highlands and Islands by Mary Beith
An excellent resource for folk traditions including the nonhuman powers of the land and animals as well as plants.

Irish Folk Ways by E. Estyn Evans
Written in the 1950s, Evans catalogues the daily and seasonal practices of homemade, ancestral, and folk skills still in use in Ireland.

Polish Traditions, Customs and Folklore by Sophie Hodorowicz Knab
A compendium of practices for each month of the year, as well as birth and death.

Resources for Pursuing Your Own Translations

The Concise Dictionary of Old Icelandic by Gier Zöega

The Bosworth-Toller Anglo-Saxon Dictionary online
http://bosworth.ff.cuni.cz/

Old English Translator
www.oldenglishtranslator.co.uk/

The Online Etymology Dictionary
www.etymonline.com/

Notes

1 Grier T. Zoëga, A Concise Old Icelandic Dictionary, 503.

2 The Bosworth-Toller Anglo-Saxon Dictionary: *http://bosworth.ff.cuni.cz.*

3 Zoëga, 343.

4 Zoëga, 88.

5 Aya Van Renterghem (2014), "The Anglo-Saxon runic poem: a critical assessment," MPhil (R) thesis, University of Glasgow; *http://theses.gla.ac.uk,* page 1, accessed November 20, 2019.

6 Ibid.

7 Ibid.

8 Jonna Louis-Jensen, "The Norwegian Runic Poem as a Mnemonic Device: The pictographic principle," Seventh International Symposium on Runes and Runic Inscriptions, University of Oslo Museum of Cultural History, 2010; *https://www.khm.uio.no/english,* page 1, accessed November 20, 2019.

9 Susan Gray, *The Woman's Book of Runes* (New York: Barnes and Noble Books), 2.

10 Adrian Poruciuc, "Old European Echoes in Germanic Runes?" *Journal of Archaeomythology* 7, (2011): 67.

11 Ibid., 68.

12 Tineke Looijenga, "Texts and Contexts of the Oldest Runic Inscriptions," Odroerir Journal Online Academic Library, (2014): 9; *http://odroerirjournal. com,* accessed November 20, 2019.

13 Ibid., 9.

14 Henry Adams Bellows, *Poetic Edda: Voluspa, www.sacred-texts.com.*

15 John Lindow, *Norse Mythology: A Guide to the Gods, Heroes, Rituals and Beliefs* (Oxford: Oxford University Press, 2001), 164.

16 "Skara Brae: The Discovery and Excavation of Orkney's Finest Neolithic Settlement, Orkneyjar," last modified February 25, 2016, *www.orkneyjar.com.*

17 Marija Gimbutas, *Civilizations of the Goddess: The World of Old Europe* (San Francisco: Harper San Francisco, 1991), vii.

18 Poruciuc, "Old European Echoes," 71.

19 Ibid., 70.

20 "Orkney Venus—early people—Scotland's History," Education Scotland; *www.educationscotland.gov.uk,* accessed May 16, 2016.

21 Max Dashu, "Woman Shaman Transcript of Disc 2: Staffs," Suppressed Histories, last modified 2013; *www.suppressedhistories.net.*

22 Snorri Sturluson, *Heimskringla,* The Online Medieval and Classical Library; *http://omacl.org.*

23 Lindow, *Norse Mythology,* 311.

24 Ibid., 50.

25 Vesta, 2020; my translation.

26 Zöega, 479.

27 Maria Kvilhaug, "Burning the Witch! – The Initiation of the Goddess and the War of the Aesir and the Vanir," *Lady of the Labyrinth´s Old Norse Mythology Website,* last update 2016, *http://freya.theladyofthelabyrinth.com.*

28 Zöega, 190.

29 Kvilhaug, "Burning the Witch!"

30 Ralph Metzner, *The Well of Remembrance: Rediscovering the Earth Wisdom Myths of Northern Europe* (Boston: Shambhala Publications, 1994), 167.

31 Lindow, *Norse Mythology,* 53.

32 Zoëga, 453.

33 Ibid., 483.

34 Ibid., 382.

35 Bellows, *Poetic Edda: Voluspa.* I use the Bellows translation here for the clear image of the giant maidens emerging from Jotunheim.

36 Zöega, 312.

37 "The Oseberg Finds," University of Oslo Museum of Cultural History, last modified December 10, 2012, *www.khm.uio.no/english.*

38 Kari Tauring, "What is a Völva?" last modified October 31, 2011, *http://karitauring.com.*

39 Ibid.

40 *Kalevala, www.sacred-texts.com.*

41 Lyle B. Steadman, Craig T. Palmer, and Christopher F. Tilley, "The Universality of Ancestor Worship," *Ethnology* 35:1 (winter 1996), 63–76.

42 Jona Lendering, "Veleda," last modified April 23, 2020; *www.livius.org.*

43 "Etymology of Old," Online Etymology Dictionary, last accessed February 17, 2020, *www.etymonline.com.*

44 Tacitus, *Germania, www.gutenberg.org*

45 *Völuspá* 16–20, *www.voluspa.org,* accessed November 20, 2019.

About the Author

Lara Veleda Vesta, MFA, is an artist, author, witch, and educator. Lara teaches at the Wild Soul School, focusing on folk magic, ancestral connection, self-initiation, and ritual practice. She is the author of *The Moon Divas Guidebook* and *The Moon Divas Oracle*. Visit her at *www.laravesta.co*.